WARS OF THE ROSES

The People, Places and Battlefields of the Yorkists and Lancastrians

Paul Kendall

FRONTLINE
BOOKS

Wars of the Roses: The People, Places and Battlefields of The Yorkists and Lancastrians

This edition published in 2023 by Frontline Books,
An imprint of Pen & Sword Books Ltd,
Yorkshire - Philadelphia

Copyright © Paul Kendall, 2023

The right of Paul Kendall to be identified as the author of this work has been asserted by him in accordance with the Copyright, Designs and Patents Act 1988.

ISBN 978 1 39909 751 2

All rights reserved. No part of this publication may be reproduced, stored in or introduced into a retrieval system, or transmitted, in any form, or by any means (electronic, mechanical, photocopying, recording or otherwise) without the prior written permission of the publisher. Any person who does any unauthorized act in relation to this publication may be liable to criminal prosecution and civil claims for damages.

CIP data records for this title are available from the British Library

Pen & Sword Books Limited incorporates the imprints of Atlas, Archaeology, Aviation, Discovery, Family History, Fiction, History, Maritime, Military, Military Classics, Politics, Select, Transport, True Crime, Air World, Frontline Publishing, Leo Cooper, Remember When, Seaforth Publishing, The Praetorian Press, Wharncliffe Local History, Wharncliffe Transport, Wharncliffe True Crime and White Owl.

PEN & SWORD BOOKS LTD
47 Church Street, Barnsley, South Yorkshire, S70 2AS, England
E-mail: enquiries@pen-and-sword.co.uk
Website: www.pen-and-sword.co.uk

Or
PEN AND SWORD BOOKS
1950 Lawrence Rd, Havertown, PA 19083, USA
E-mail: Uspen-and-sword@casematepublishers.com

For more information on our books, please visit www.frontline-books.com, email info@frontline-books.com or write to us at the above address.

Printed and bound in the UK by CPI Group (UK) Ltd.

Typeset in 10/14pt Adobe Caslon by SJmagic DESIGN SERVICES, India.

Contents

Introduction 8
Acknowledgements 11

The places and objects that represent the Wars of the Roses

1 Effigy Head of Henry V 12
2 The Talbot Shrewsbury Book depicting the enthronement of Henry VI 14
3 Notre-Dame de Paris (Our Lady of Paris) 16
4 Statue of Henry VI, the King's Screen, York Minster 19
5 Joan of Arc Tower, Rouen 21
6 Titchfield Abbey 23
7 Tomb of Humphrey, Duke of Gloucester 25
8 The London Stone 27
9 Fotheringhay Castle 30
10 Statue of Margaret of Anjou, Angers 32
11 Statue of Henry VI 34
12 Windsor Castle 35
13 Engraving depicting Westminster 37
14 Clocktower, St Albans 39
15 Map of St Albans in 1455 42
16 Plaque commemorating Edmund Beaufort, 2nd Duke of Somerset ...44
17 St Albans Cathedral and Abbey Gatehouse 47
18 Pembroke Castle 51
19 The ragged staff emblem 53
20 Audley's Cross, Blore Heath 55
21 Ludlow Castle 58
22 Ludford Bridge 60
23 Sandwich Quay 62
24 Eleanor Cross, Northampton 64
25 The Tower of London 66
26 The Painted Chamber, Westminster Palace 68
27 Sandal Castle, Wakefield 71

28	Battlefield at Wakefield	74
29	Monument dedicated to Richard, 3rd Duke of York, Wakefield	76
30	Old Wakefield Bridge	78
31	Micklegate Bar, York	80
32	Battle of Mortimer's Cross Monument	82
33	Marketplace at St Albans	85
34	Crossing at Ferrybridge	88
35	St Mary's Church, Lead	90
36	Towton Memorial Cross	91
37	Bloody Meadow, Towton	93
38	Wooden bridge over the Cock Beck, Towton	95
39	The Towton Skeleton	97
40	All Saints Church, Saxton & Lord Dacre's Tomb	99
41	Chapel of St John the Evangelist, Tower of London	102
42	Westminster Abbey	104
43	Execution site, Tower Hill, London	106
44	Bamburgh Castle	109
45	Reading Abbey	112
46	Waddington Old Hall	114
47	Danesmoor, site of the Battle of Edgcote	116
48	Battle of Losecoat Field Monument	118
49	Angers Cathedral	120
50	Compass Memorial, Purfleet Quay, King's Lynn	123
51	Edward IV & Richard, Duke of Gloucester (Richard III), plaque, Cromer	126
52	Walmgate Bar, York	129
53	Battle of Barnet Obelisk	131
54	Statue of Margaret of Anjou and Prince Edward, Paris	134
55	Gupshill Manor, Tewkesbury	136
56	Ghent Manuscript, depiction of the Battle of Tewkesbury	137
57	Bloody Meadow, Tewkesbury	139
58	Burial site of Prince Edward, Tewkesbury Abbey	141
59	Tewkesbury Abbey	144
60	Model of the medieval London Bridge	147
61	The King's Private Chapel, the Wakefield Tower	151
62	Engraving of Henry VI	155
63	Stained glass window commemorating marriage of Richard, Duke of Gloucester, and Anne Neville.	157
64	Church of St Mary and All Saints, Fotheringhay	159

65	Yorkist Heraldry	162
66	Bowyer Tower	165
67	Engraving of Edward IV	167
68	Eltham Palace	169
69	St George's Chapel, Windsor Castle	171
70	Rose and Crown Inn, Stony Stratford	173
71	Crosby Hall	176
72	Entrance to Westminster Abbey	178
73	St Paul's Cross, London	180
74	Baynard's Castle, London	182
75	The Coronation Chair	184
76	Westminster Hall	186
77	Arms of Richard III, Charter of Incorporation Plaque, Gloucester	188
78	York Minster	190
79	Archbishop's Palace, York	192
80	The Bloody Tower, Tower of London	195
81	Staircase where two skeletons were discovered	197
82	Facial Reconstruction of Richard III	200
83	Middleham Castle	202
84	Nottingham Castle	204
85	Mill Bay Memorial	206
86	Henry Tudor House, Shrewsbury	209
87	Blue Boar Inn, Leicester	211
88	Bow Bridge, Leicester	213
89	King Dick's Well, Bosworth	216
90	Bosworth Battlefield Site, Fenn Lane, and the Bosworth Boar	218
91	Statue of Richard III, Leicester	221
92	Sundial Memorial, Bosworth	223
93	The Two Kings' Plaque, Leicester	225
94	Turret gateway entrance to Leicester Castle	227
95	A royal grave, Greyfriars, Leicester	228
96	Skeleton of Richard III	230
97	Tomb of Richard III	232
98	Rose Window, York Minster	234
99	Gatehouse of Richmond Palace	236
100	Tomb of Henry VII and Elizabeth Tudor	238

Bibliography 240

Introduction

The Wars of the Roses divided Britain during the fifteenth century. The crown of England exchanged hands six times between the Yorkists and Lancastrians as they fought to assert their right to rule. The Yorkist defeat at Bosworth ended the Plantagenet dynasty and saw the emergence of the Tudors. This volume chronicles this turbulent and violent episode in English history.

At the time of the conflict, it was known as the 'Cousins' War', for it was a war fought between the descendants of the sons of Edward III (who reigned from 1327 until 1377) and Philippa of Hainault; the sons being, John of Gaunt, Duke of Lancaster, representing the Lancastrians and Lionel, Duke of Clarence, being from the House of York. Tensions between the rival Houses of Lancaster and York was ignited when Henry Bolingbroke, son of John of Gaunt, usurped Richard II's crown in 1399. Richard II was the legitimate heir, being the son of Edward, the Black Prince, the first son of Edward III. Bolingbroke would become Henry IV, first king of the House of Lancaster, and reign until 1413, when he was succeeded by his son Henry V, who became the victor of Agincourt and brought stability. Although the fuse for the Wars of the Roses was lit in 1399, it would take a further fifty years before their dispute escalated into violence at the first battle, which took place at St Albans on 22 May 1455.

The main protagonists around the time of action at St Albans were Richard Plantagenet, 3rd Duke of York, representing the Yorkists, and his cousin, Henry VI, the figurehead of the House of Lancaster. York would engage in battle at St Albans with the Lancastrian army led by Henry VI, the great-grandson of John of Gaunt, the third son of Edward III. Through the male line, York was the grandson of Edmund of Langley, 1st Duke of York, and fifth son of Edward III. He also had a stronger claim through the line of his mother, Anne Mortimer, daughter of the Earl of March, as he was the great-great grandson of Lionel, Duke of Clarence, the second son of Edward III. Clarence was the next in the line of succession following the death of his older brother, Edward, the Black Prince, while Henry VI's claim to the throne was further weakened because he was a descendent of Clarence's younger brother, John of Gaunt, and that the line of descent was tarnished by his grandfather Henry Bolingbroke, who had undermined that link through his usurpation of Richard II to become Henry IV.

The Wars of the Roses were essentially a family blood feud, and the words that John Clifford, 9th Baron Clifford, spoke to Edmund, Earl of Rutland, on Old Wakefield Bridge in 1460 before he plunged a dagger through his heart, resonate throughout the conflict. He said, 'By God's blood, thy father slew mine, and so will I do thee and all thy kin.' Clifford was avenging the death of his father at St Albans in 1455 and battles from Wakefield onwards would conclude with the execution or murder of lords for whom a family had a grievance or a feud.

Richard, 3rd Duke of York, was a wealthy and powerful man, who inherited from his father, Richard, Earl of Cambridge, the title of Duke of York together with the earldoms of Cambridge and Rutland. He was aged 4 when his father was executed for plotting against Henry V in 1415. Cambridge's brother, Edward, was killed at Agincourt in 1415 and the title Duke of York passed to Richard. Through his mother, Ann Mortimer, he inherited the earldom of March and the Welsh borders, together with the earldoms of Clare, Connaught and Trim. Richard would become the wealthiest nobleman in England, second to the sovereign. If Henry VI had died without leaving an heir, York would certainly have been crowned king, for there was no other nobleman who had a stronger claim to the throne.

The Wars of the Roses were fought during thirty years between 1455 until 1471, resuming in 1485 until 1487, which marked a turbulent part in English history. The battles were brief and between 1471 to 1485 marked a period of peace when no battles were fought.

The name given to the 'Wars of the Roses' is a fallacy for which Shakespeare helped to ferment the misconception with the fictional scene that he wrote for Henry IV Part I, Act II, Scene IV, where the nobles from the House of York and Lancaster picked a rose to choose a side in Temple Gardens in London. It was not until the nineteenth century that Sir Walter Scott referred to the 'Wars of the Roses' in his novel *Anne of Geierstein*, in reference to the colours of the roses, red for the Lancastrians and white for the Yorkists. During his youth, Edward IV was often referred to as the 'rose of Rouen', and the white rose was adopted of the emblem of the House of York and represented the cause of civil and religious freedom during the war, but no rose was attributed to the Lancastrian cause during the conflict. It was only after the war had ended that Henry VII created the Tudor Rose, where red roses represented Henry's rightful claim to the throne through his association with the Dukes of Lancaster and the white roses signifying the house of York were incorporated within the design.

England was a country that lacked order, justice, or strong government. Lawlessness among the nobility and family feuds were unchecked and allowed to escalate. The ruling classes had fought in the Hundred Years' War in France and had profited from plundering its assets. The French eventually liberated their own land and the English nobility returned home demoralised. Without an occupation, they then turned their weapons upon themselves. These complex issues created an environment that descended into civil war.

Although the conflict was between the Houses of York and Lancashire, their support did not totally come from the counties in which their dynastic families were named. Strong support for the House of Lancashire was evident in Yorkshire, Northumberland and south-western counties, while the House of York was dominant in the Midlands, London and Kent.

The conflict affected the reigns of five kings between 1422 and 1487. The Lancastrian Henry VI reigned from 1422 to 1461 and again from 1470 to 1471; The Yorkist Edward IV seized the throne from him during 1461. He was usurped in 1470 and was restored as monarch in 1471, reigning until 1483. His successor, Edward V, reigned briefly from 9 April to 26 June

1483, but was never crowned. In dubious circumstances, his Yorkist uncle, Richard, Duke of Gloucester, took the crown and reigned as Richard III for two years until 1485, when after his death on the battlefield at Bosworth, Henry Tudor ascended the throne as Henry VII. These monarchs had the support of strong women such as Margaret of Anjou, Henry VI's queen; Elizabeth Woodville, the commoner who married Edward IV; and Margaret Beaufort, the mother of Henry VII, whose ambition for her son was boundless, and their roles make the story of the Wars of the Roses enthralling to read.

The war would account for the deaths of three English kings, all slain: Henry VI, Edward V and Richard III; and would destroy the House of Plantagenet, which had reigned for 331 years starting from 1154. It decimated the nobility, with the deaths of twenty-four barons, seventeen earls, twelve dukes, one marquis and one viscount.[1] Three Dukes of Somerset were killed during the war: Edmund (2nd Duke), was killed at St Albans; his son, Henry (3rd Duke), was captured at Hexham and beheaded; while the 4th Duke, Edmund, was captured and executed at Tewkesbury. Two Earls of Northumberland were also killed; Henry Percy (2nd Earl) died at St Albans while his son, also named Henry, (3rd Earl) died at Towton. Richard Neville, Warwick the Kingmaker and his brother, John Neville, Marquis of Montagu, were both killed at Barnet.

The Wars of the Roses served as a lesson in kingship, beginning with a weakened, passive and good-natured Henry VI, who was regarded as an imbecile. His failure to make a decision, take control and lead his country created a power vacuum that incited challengers such as Richard of York to contend his throne. Although he did not achieve his aspirations of becoming king, Richard would be the father of two kings, Edward IV and Richard III, and the grandfather of Edward V. Edward, Earl of March, would prove himself in battle as a warrior and a commander in the battles of Mortimer's Cross and Towton before becoming Edward IV, achieved by the time he was 19. Twice he seized the throne, and on two occasions he had to flee in exile, but after the death of Henry VI, Edward rebuilt the monarchy and strengthened the nation's economy during his reign, which would lay the foundations for the Tudor dynasty to flourish. His marriage to a widowed commoner, Elizabeth Woodville, whose husband had fought on the opposing side, and his overindulgence for wine and mistresses made Edward IV an intriguing monarch. However, his reign would end in tragedy with the disappearance of his sons, Edward V and Richard, Duke of York.

Richard III is an enigmatic and complex figure who has caused much dispute amongst historians during the past 500 years. His motto 'Loyalty binds me' is apt, because he devoted most part of his life to supporting his brother, Edward IV. He was a military commander by the time he was 19, who had demonstrated that he was an able strategist, fearless and courageous at the battles of Barnet and Tewkesbury. At the age of 31 he had usurped his nephew's throne and became one of England's most controversial monarchs. During the early part of his life little is known about him. He was the youngest son of Richard, Duke of York, and was not expected to ascend to the throne of England. On 12 October 1462, Edward IV conferred honours and

---

1. Halstead, Caroline A., *Richard III*, Volume One (Longman, London, 1844), p.32.

titles upon his brother Richard, aged 10, making him Duke of Gloucester and electing him to the Order of the Garter. Richard became a soldier and administrator who was content in governing the north of England. He came to prominence when Edward IV died and caused much intrigue regarding the circumstances behind Richard's claim to the throne, and whether he was directly responsible for the deaths of his nephews. The Tudor propaganda machine ensured that history would regard him as the deformed, maligned villain who murdered them, but in recent years, perception of Richard III the man has been reviewed and revised. The Richard III Society, established in 1924, has devoted itself to championing his innocence. He was no worse than other individuals during his era. The world was a brutal, savage place where violence was the predominate means to secure one's own position and endure in a lawless society. Richard III was indeed a man of his time.

As control of the throne changed hands, so did the loyalties of noble families, where they changed allegiances if it preserved their wealth and lives. The story of the Wars of the Roses is a tale of woe and treachery, interwoven with the stories of ruthless, powerful individuals, who were callous and brutal to exploit the conflict for their own survival and wealth. They were men such as Richard Neville, 16th Earl of Warwick, who played a prominent role in the disposition of two monarchs as he changed his allegiances, earning the name 'Kingmaker'. The fortunes of families depended on whether their allegiances were aligned with the current ruling king. Those families who challenged the king who were suspected of treason were punished with their titles and estates seized and passed to loyal families.

This book serves as a journey back to the Wars of the Roses through places and objects, where each location, object, item or monument provides a snapshot of its relevance to the conflict, at the same time telling that story in chronological order.

Paul Kendall
Folkestone 2022

Acknowledgements

I thank Bill James, churchwarden at the Church of St Mary and All Saints, Fotheringhay, for guiding me around the church during my visit in 2017 in preparation for this book. I thank Martin Mace and John Grehan for giving me the opportunity to write this book and their encouragement, and Robert Mitchell for his help with the many images that follow. I also thank my partner, Tricia Newsome, for her support in all my projects.

1
Effigy Head of Henry V

The infant Henry VI succeeded Henry V to the English throne.

During the summer 1421, Henry V left his pregnant wife, Catherine de Valois, for France to fight against Charles VII, her brother, for the French throne. On 6 December 1421, Catherine gave birth to Henry VI at Windsor Castle. Nine months later, Henry V died and was buried in Westminster Abbey.

Henry V was besieging the French town Meaux when he heard the news of the birth of his son. He sent a message back to Windsor Castle instructing Catherine to christen their son, which took place at St George's Chapel. During June 1422, Catherine left Henry VI in the care of his uncle, Humphrey, Duke of Gloucester, while she joined her husband in France. Henry VI would never meet his father, because he died of dysentery, aged 35 at the Château de Vincennes on 31 August 1422. Accompanied by his widow, the remains of Henry V were brought from France to London, where he was buried on 7 November 1422 in a lavish funeral in Westminster Abbey.

Henry VI ascended the throne aged 9 months old to become the youngest successor to the English crown. Seven weeks later, on 21 October 1422, his grandfather, Charles VI, died, and Henry VI succeeded him as King of France in accordance with the Treaty of Troyes agreed in 1420, which stipulated that the heirs of Henry V would succeed to the French throne. The people of France much preferred the Dauphin, Charles, to succeed his father, but the duchy of Burgundy held the power, enforced the treaty and was strongly aligned to England. This was an unprecedented and alarming situation because a 10-month-old baby, Henry VI, was sovereign of two nations. Henry was unable to choose his ministers, advisors or make decisions regarding matters of state.

Prior to his death, Henry V had made provisions in his will for the governing of both England and France. Catherine de Valois was not granted powers to rule England while her son was an infant, therefore the late king had decreed that a regency council comprising of seventeen noblemen and religious leaders should govern. His brothers would play a prominent role in that regency. Humphrey, Duke of Gloucester, was appointed Lord Protector and Regent of England, and John of Lancaster, 1st Duke of Bedford, became the Regent of France and Governor of Normandy. Thomas Beaufort, Duke of Exeter, and Cardinal Henry Beaufort,

Tomb of Henry V in Westminster Abbey. After his death at Vincennes in France on 31 August 1422, his remains were embalmed and lay in Rouen Cathedral before they were transported to England. His funeral took place at Westminster Abbey on 7 November 1422. (Copyright Dean and Chapter of Westminster)

uncles of Henry V, were appointed tutors and governors of the boy king alongside Richard Beauchamp, 13th Earl of Warwick. The regency was established on 9 December 1422 and governed England while Henry VI was a child. This marked the beginning of the longest period of royal minority in English history and would last for fifteen years until 1437.

2

The Talbot Shrewsbury Book depicting the enthronement of Henry VI

Henry VI crowned King of England at Westminster Abbey.

France was a divided nation, with Charles VII reigning south of the River Loire, while the English governed alongside their Burgundian allies ruled north of the Loire. The French Army, commanded by Joan of Arc, broke the siege of Orléans on 8 May 1429 and this marked the first French victory over the English since the defeat at Agincourt in 1415. It also allowed Charles VII, who was uncle and rival to Henry VI, to break through the English lines to be crowned King of France at Reims Cathedral on 29 July 1429, which made the requirement to crown Henry VI more urgent.

The Regency Council in England was divided regarding the continuation of the Hundred Years' War with France. The insurgency led by Joan of Arc and the coronation of Charles VII demonstrated that the French would resist the English occupation of France and was regarded as a direct challenge to the English king, who was aged 7 and had not been crowned in either England or France. John, Duke of Bedford, sent a message from France to the Regency Council that it was imperative for Henry VI to be crowned in France in the hope of strengthening English dominance in France. This provoked a sense of urgency, but before this could happen, he needed to be initially crowned as King of England. Parliament was summoned and the date for his coronation was arranged for 6 November 1429. The streets were lined with spectators as they watched the procession of Henry VI as it proceeded through London. A priest and several other individuals were crushed to death due to the immense crowds.

Henry VI wore 'a cloth of scharlet furryde',[2] and he was carried into Westminster Abbey by Richard Beauchamp, 13th Earl of Warwick. The king was taken to a scaffold that had been built between the choir and the high altar. William Gregory wrote that 'there the king was

---

2. Gairdner, James, *Three Fifteenth-Century Chronicles* (Camden Society, 1880), p.165.

Henry VI enthroned; detail of a miniature from the Talbot Shrewsbury Book. (British Library)

sat in the middle of the scaffold there, beholding the people all about sadly and wisely'.[3] Only part of the ceremony was performed by his great uncle, Cardinal Henry Beaufort, Bishop of Winchester, with the remainder required to be conducted in France. When the heavy Crown of St Edward was placed upon his head, two bishops stood on each side of the boy to support him while he wore it.

3. Ibid., p.165.

3

Notre-Dame de Paris (Our Lady of Paris)

Henry VI crowned King of France.

On 16 December 1431, Henry VI, aged 10, became the only English sovereign to be crowned King of France.

It was the tradition for the coronation of French sovereigns to take place at Reims Cathedral, but because it was held by the French, the ceremony had to take place at Notre-Dame de Paris. The French chronicler Enguerrand de Monstrelet wrote:

> that he went from the palace in great pomp, and attended by a numerous body of nobles and ecclesiastics, to the church of Notre Dame, for his coronation. In the nave of the church had been erected a scaffold eight score feet long, and of a proper height, which was ascended from the nave, and led to the entrance of the choir. The king was crowned by the cardinal of Winchester [Cardinal Henry Beaufort], who also chanted the mass, to the great displeasure of the bishop of Paris, who said that the office belonged to him. At the offertory the king made an offering of bread and wine in the usual manner. The wine was in a huge pot of silver gilt, which was seized on by the king's officers, to the discontent of the canons of the cathedral, who claimed it as their prerequisite and they urged their complaints before the king and council, who, after it had cost them much in this claim, caused it to be returned to them.[4]

The coronation at Notre-Dame de Paris did not cement English authority and during the reign of Henry VI the English eventually lost control. On 29 January 1432, Henry VI's one and only visit to France came to an end when he sailed from Calais for Dover. A peace policy was instigated in 1432, but there were further splits in the regency. The English government was in capable hands so long as John, Duke of Bedford, was a prominent member of the regency, but when he died on 14 September 1435, and combined with the added complexity of England's

---

4. Monstrelet, Enguerrand de, *The Chronicles of Enguerrand de Monstrelet* (H.G. Bohn, London, 1853), p.597.

Above: Notre-Dame de Paris. Sadly, on 15 April 2019 the cathedral caught fire and sustained significant damage to its structure, including the destruction of the roof. (Luciano Mortula/Shutterstock)

Right: The coronation of Henry VI, aged 10. He was crowned in Westminster Abbey and Notre-Dame de Paris. (Author's collection)

NOTRE-DAME DE PARIS (OUR LADY OF PARIS) 17

ally, the Duke of Burgundy, defecting to the French side, England's ability to maintain control of occupied France began to diminish and the regency was divided into two factions. Cardinal Henry Beaufort and William de la Pole, 1st Duke of Suffolk, led one group who advocated peace, while the other was led by the king's uncle, Humphrey, Duke of Gloucester, and his cousin, Richard, 3rd Duke of York, who opposed peace with France and would later challenge Henry for the crown of England. Aristocratic families were also competing for the benefits of political power within the regions, which would cause further dissension across the kingdom. The failure to retain occupied territory in France occurred before Henry VI reached adulthood and combined with the inability to control the feuding families were among the causes that would ignite the Wars of the Roses.

4

Statue of Henry VI, the King's Screen, York Minster

The stone screen, known as the King's Screen or Quire Screen, that separates the Quire and the Sanctuary from the nave within York Minster contains fifteen statues of English monarchs that reigned during the Norman and Medieval period in history, including Henry VI.

Henry VI attended his first council meeting on 1 October 1435, aged 14, and he started to sign off petitions during May 1436. His mother, Catherine de Valois, had married Sir Owen Tudor, but she died on 3 January 1437. Henry would assume complete royal authority in December 1437 when he reached his sixteenth birthday, to fulfil his responsibilities as King of England and France.

A nation bankrupted, divisions within his council, an aristocracy that was growing powerful and could not be restrained, a corrupt legal system and a conflict with France that could not be won, and continued to be a burden financially, were among the problems that Henry VI had inherited as king. However, he was devoid of intelligence, lacked experience to make decisions that addressed the national problems and authorised actions that were damaging to the Crown, such as sanctioning requests that would leave him and the nation financially disadvantaged. Although educated, he was foolish, incompetent, unworldly, even simple minded, and made grave errors of judgement. He surrounded himself with advisors more concerned with serving themselves than their king as they manipulated him into making decisions where they would benefit financially.

Life within a religious order would have suited Henry VI instead of being sovereign. His confessor, John Blacman, wrote that he was 'a diligent and sincere worshipper of God was this king, more given to God and to devout prayer than to handling worldly and temporal things, or practising vain sports or pursuits: these he despised as trifling, and was continually occupied either in prayer or in reading of the scriptures.'[5]

The Battle of Castillon, fought in 1453, signified the end of the Hundred Years' War between France and England and resulted in the loss of the majority of land gained by the English, except for Calais. Henry was ill-equipped to deal with the nation's adversaries. He was weak, indecisive and incapable of making decisions in a crisis. His spiritual temperament and

---

5. James, M.E., *Henry VI, A Reprint of John Blacman's Memoir* (University of Cambridge, 1919), p.27.

Statue of Henry VI in the King's Screen, York Minster. (Author's collection)

inability to confront and deal with his opponents created a power vacuum, an environment where aristocratic families took advantage to further their own agendas and establish their dominance within the King's council to increase their power, influence and wealth. This caused tensions and disagreements with rival factions and families within England. Henry VI was unable to control this situation and it eventually resulted in open revolt.

5

Joan of Arc Tower, Rouen

Surviving remnant of Rouen Castle, birthplace of Edward IV.

Rouen was captured by Henry V in 1419 during the Hundred Years' War and it was held by the English until 1449. This circular tower is the only surviving part of Rouen Castle, which was formed of an impregnable circular wall with ten towers, surrounded by a moat.

It was at Rouen Castle that Joan of Arc was tried on 9 May 1431. Nine years later, on 2 July 1440, Henry VI appointed Richard, 3rd Duke of York, as Lieutenant of France; an appointment scheduled to last five years. His wife, Cecily Neville, did not want to separate from her husband for that length of time, so she decided to accompany him. The Yorks arrived in Rouen during June 1441 and Richard led a successful campaign to relive the town of Pontoise, which had been besieged by Charles VII. During the following year, Cecily gave birth to Edward on 28 April 1442 at Rouen Castle and he was baptized in the chapel within the castle. Cecily had previously given birth to Anna at Fotheringhay Castle in 1439 and to a son, Henry, in 1441, but he died, so Edward became York's heir. More siblings were born at Rouen Castle, including Edmund, Earl of Rutland, born on 17 May 1443, and Elizabeth, born on 22 April 1444. A French woman, Anne of Caux, was hired as Edward's nurse and she accompanied the York family when they returned to England, continuing to look after him. When Edward ascended the throne seventeen years later, Anne was granted an annual pension, which was honoured after his death by his brother Richard III.

On 18 March 1445, York met his future adversary, Margaret of Anjou, at Pontoise and escorted her on part of her journey through France to Harfleur, where she boarded a ship that would take her to England and her wedding to Henry VI. During that journey they stayed at Rouen Castle, where Margaret was received by Cecily. Her future husband arranged for Margaret to arrive in Rouen on a chariot, but she was too ill to participate in the ceremony planned.

Although it was never questioned at the time of Edward's birth, Cecily became the victim of slanderous speculation years later that her husband was not the father of Edward, who allegedly resembled a French archer that was stationed in Rouen. This accusation was never substantiated, but her younger son, Richard, would exploit this despicable charge several decades later when providing his own claim to the English throne.

Joan of Arc Tower, the only surviving remnant of Rouen Castle. (Hindrik Johannes de Groot/ Shutterstock)

6
Titchfield Abbey

Henry VI married Margaret of Anjou.

The wedding ceremony of Henry VI and Margaret of Anjou took place at Titchfield Abbey in Hampshire on 23 April 1445.

William de la Pole, the 1st Earl of Suffolk, became close advisor to Henry VI when he was appointed Steward of the Household in 1440 and during April 1444, in an initiative to bring the Hundred Years' War to a conclusion, he negotiated the marriage between Henry VI, who was aged 23, with Margaret of Anjou, the 14-year-old niece of Charles VII.

Margaret's father, René, Duke of Anjou, was impoverished, with his possessions and estates occupied by the English. It was agreed that Henry VI would relinquish Margaret's dowry and pay the expenses for the wedding through the English exchequer. During May 1444, Suffolk signed the Treaty of Tours on behalf of Henry VI, with the French envoys representing Charles VII. The treaty guaranteed a two-year truce, the betrothal of Margaret to Henry VI, as well as a secret clause whereby the English would relinquish control of the territories of Anjou and Maine to Margaret's father, while England retained the territories of Normandy and Aquitaine.

Margaret of Anjou sailed from Cherbourg aboard the small English vessel the *Cocke John*, which after a turbulent passage entered Portsmouth Harbour and landed at Portchester on 9 April 1445. The wedding was meant to have taken place at Windsor, but because Margaret was recovering from ill health it took place at Titchfield Abbey on 23 April. Lords and ladies travelled from London and Windsor to attend the marriage ceremony, which was officiated by William Aiscough, the Bishop of Salisbury. After the ceremony, Margaret was presented with a lion as a wedding gift. In the book of expenses for the wedding, payments were made to two men, who fed the lion and transferred it to the royal menagerie at the Tower of London, where it was kept.[6]

The newly wedded couple remained at Titchfield Abbey for several days. Bishop Aiscough warned the king to refrain from physical pleasures, no more than necessary to produce an heir.

---

6. Abbott, Jacob, *Margaret of Anjou* (Harper & Brothers Publishers, London, 1902), p.109.

Titchfield Abbey. (Courtesy of Adam Grenough; via Wikimedia Commons)

Henry took heed of the bishop's advice and this may be the reason why Margaret did not produce an heir until eight years later.

Margaret was beautiful and articulate, and her marriage to Henry VI brought hope of an heir and lasting peace between England and France. Her native tongue was French and she had to learn to speak English. She was received warmly when she arrived in London on 28 May 1445, two days prior to her coronation in Westminster Abbey. After the marriage it was realised that Suffolk had negotiated a bad deal. Margaret's popularity declined, but she loyally stood by her husband's side, championed his right to reign and strongly resented his enemies, especially the House of York. The Treaty of Tours, and in particular the arranged marriage, was a major diplomatic failure for Henry VI because hostilities with France resumed in 1449, resulting in England losing further territories. It was one of the principal causes that angered English nobles and acted as a catalyst for the beginning of the Wars of the Roses.

7

Tomb of Humphrey, Duke of Gloucester

Gloucester died and was buried at St Albans Cathedral.

Gloucester fought at Agincourt alongside his brother, Henry V, in 1415 and in the conquest of Normandy during 1417–19.

Gloucester was regarded as a patron of the arts and supported education. He founded the first public library at Oxford, which is now known as the Bodleian Library. He served as Lord Protector to his nephew, Henry VI, during his minority. He quarrelled with his brother, John, Duke of Bedford, and Cardinal Henry Beaufort, who formed the part of the regency vehemently opposing peace with France. Gloucester lost his influence in court when the minority of Henry VI ended. When it was learnt that part of Henry's marriage agreement meant the return of Anjou and Maine to the French, he became angry and openly voiced his opposition, quarrelling with his nephew. His stance was misconstrued as a direct challenge to the king and Margaret, in allegiance with Suffolk, persuaded Henry to order the arrest of his uncle during early 1447 on a charge of treason, which was a false accusation. Gloucester died soon after on 23 February 1447, from natural causes, perhaps apoplexy brought on by the anxiety caused by his arrest. He was buried in a small memorial chapel beneath St Albans Shrine, the only member of the royal family to be buried in St Albans Cathedral. His estates were given to Queen Margaret.

Gloucester's death would herald concerns for the throne of England. Henry VI had no son and given that Gloucester had no children, it meant that Richard, 3rd Duke of York, was the next in the line of succession. This placed York in a dangerous situation, for he too shared Gloucester's view of retaining and defending English-occupied France instead of relinquishing it. He favoured an aggressive policy towards France and was concerned about the corrupt and inept officials advising the king. York was willing to champion the cause for removing those advisors and reforming government.

York's political views would place him on a collision course with Queen Margaret and the king's advisers, Edmund Beaufort, 2nd Duke of Somerset, and William de la Pole, the 1st Earl of Suffolk. York was Henry's principal commander in France and despite his strong royal lineage he felt excluded from the royal councils and that his position was surpassed by Somerset, whom he loathed. York was concerned that the control he exerted would have a detrimental effect upon England. Bad accounting meant that Henry VI was unable to pay his army in Normandy, including York, who was refused payment while Somerset was able to access whatever funds were available. Eventually, Henry VI had to pawn some of his jewels in order to pay outstanding debts. York also feared that Henry VI would declare Somerset as his heir.

At the instigation of Suffolk, Henry appointed York as Lieutenant of Ireland for a tenure of ten years during July 1447. York was unofficially banished in exile in order to keep him away from the council. While he was in Ireland, Henry VI and his advisers continued to make poor decisions and lose the confidence of the populace, which resulted in some parts of the population looking towards York for strong leadership. In order to achieve that objective, he recognised that he must not fall into the same trap that befell Gloucester; York must publicly appear loyal as he set about removing the negative influences surrounding the king. When York returned to England and to the council after Cade's rebellion in 1450, the discord between York and Somerset continued.

Above left: Plaque denoting the tomb of Humphrey, Duke of Gloucester, at St Albans Cathedral. (Author's collection)

Above right: The chapel containing the remains of Humphrey, Duke of Gloucester, can be seen through the grating adjacent to the plaque. (Author's collection)

26 WARS OF THE ROSES – THE PEOPLE, PLACES AND BATTLEFIELDS

8

The London Stone

Dissension in London.

The remaining part of the London Stone is now located at 111 Cannon Street. It was originally situated in the middle of Cannon Street and is believed to be of Roman origin, but its purpose is unknown. It was known as the 'London Stone' in the twelfth century and was regarded as a prominent city landmark. During Jack Cade's rebellion in July 1450, Cade struck this stone with his sword and announced that he was the Lord of London.

Dissatisfied with the bad governance of Henry VI, Jack Cade had assembled an army in Kent during April to June 1450 and revolted against the abuses of power, malpractices of corrupt officials, failure of justice, and the loss of English-occupied territory in France. The king, advised by his ministers, had given away Crown lands and its new owners profited from the revenue generated, which resulted in the king becoming dependent upon the Commons by oppressing them with heavy taxation to cover his own expenses. The country was bankrupt to the extent that Richard, Duke of York, in his role as Lord Lieutenant of Ireland, had received no pay from Henry VI between 1448 until autumn 1450, even though he had effectively governed Ireland. All the king could offer was to permit York to export wool to Calais without the need to pay custom charges for a year. The revolt led by Jack Cade, known as the 'Captain of Kent', was the largest insurgence during the fifteenth century. Cade and his followers were royalists and the rebellion was not directed against the king, but against his advisors. It saw the assassination of the king's close minister, William de la Pole, 1st Duke of Suffolk, who led a disastrous military campaign in France. His ship was intercepted in the English Channel and his decapitated body was found dumped on the beach at Dover, next to his head. The insurgency also resulted in the murder of William Aiscough, the Bishop of Salisbury, because he had married Henry VI and his unpopular wife, Margaret of Anjou.

After defeating Sir Humphrey Stafford at Solefield, Cade led his army to Southwark on 2 July 1450, where he set up quarters in the White Hart Inn. Henry VI had been residing in St John's Priory, Clerkenwell, and fled to Kenilworth. During the following day, Cade charged across the old medieval London Bridge wearing armour. He struck the London Stone with his sword and asserted that he was in control of the city.

On 4 July 1450, James Fiennes, Lord Saye, the former Treasurer, was brought before Cade, tried for supporting Suffolk at London Guildhall and executed at Cheapside, with his head placed upon London Bridge.

Cade was unable to control his men when they started to ransack London and the cause of removing the corrupt ministers was lost as Londoners turned against them. They engaged Cade's forces in battle on London Bridge, which was retaken on 5 July. Queen Margaret, who remained in Greenwich, intervened during the following day by sending religious leaders into the city with offers of pardons to the insurgents if they dispersed from London. A large proportion of the rebels took this opportunity and withdrew from the city. Cade became a fugitive with a price on his head. He was eventually caught on 12 July 1450 and mortally wounded at Heathfield, East Sussex. His remains were returned to London, where he was decapitated and his head placed on London Bridge, facing Kent.

During July 1450, Somerset had surrendered Caen and Normandy to the French, together with his artillery. York was furious and wrote to the king advising that Somerset should be arraigned as a traitor. However, Queen Margaret supported Somerset completely. A month after he returned to London, on 11 September 1450, Henry VI appointed the unpopular

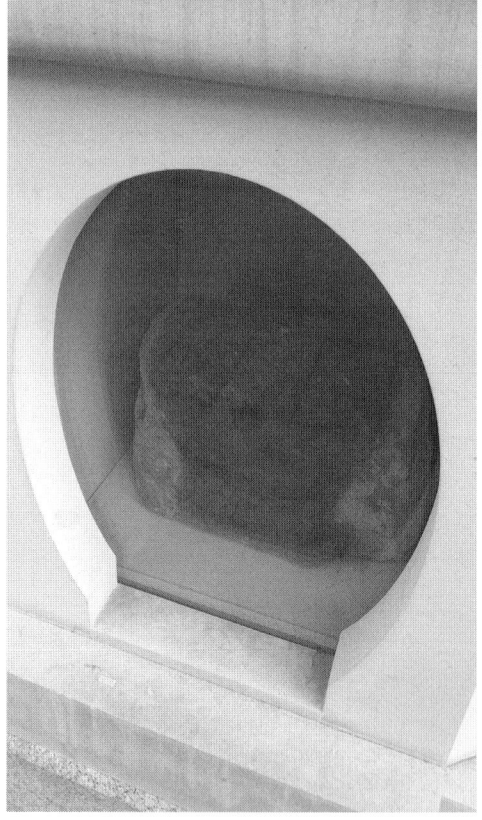

Above left and above right: The London Stone. (Author's collection)

Somerset as Constable of England, signalling that the corrupt regime would continue, much to the detriment of those who had revolted in England and Richard, 3rd Duke of York, who was in Ireland.

Although Cade's rebellion had failed, it motivated York to return from Ireland to England without the king's permission. York arrived in London during September 1450. In order to initiate the removal of incompetent advisors, he had to get within the king's circle, so he declared himself to be the king's true liegeman and servant in Westminster Palace. In an act of appeasement, Henry VI appointed York as one of his councillors, and from this position he was able to institute reforms to Parliament. He encouraged its members to petition the king to remove thirty of his advisors, including the unpopular minister Somerset, from his council of advisors, and to declare York his heir. Henry complied with the removal of some of his advisors except for Somerset, which would create a volatile situation between the bitter rivals, Somerset and York. Henry and Margaret felt threatened by York, and Somerset had to remain in order to resist him. Henry also rejected Parliament's proposal to proclaim York as heir.

The London Stone is a physical reminder of Jack Cade's revolt. The stone was relocated to the north of Cannon Street and set in an alcove within the wall of St Swithin's Church on this site. Although the church was severely damaged during the Second World War and demolished during 1961–62, the London Stone was incorporated within the design of a new office building at 111 Cannon Street. The stone was placed in its current location in 2018.

9
Fotheringhay Castle

Birthplace of Richard III.

A castle was built at Fotheringhay on the banks of the River Nene, in Northamptonshire, c.1100 by Simon de Senlis, the Norman Earl of Northampton and Huntingdon. After he died, Maud, his widow, married David, King of Scotland, and possession of the castle passed down to the Scottish line of succession. The castle became the principal administrative centre for the House of York and a royal palace during the fifteenth century. The castle was enlarged and strengthened by Edmund of Langley, 1st Duke of York, the sixth child of Edward III. The River Nene formed a natural defence of the southern walls of Fotheringhay Castle, while the other sides were protected by a moat. The motte and a piece of masonry is all that remains.

Fotheringhay Castle became the favourite residence of Richard, 3rd Duke of York, and his wife, Cecily Neville. It was here that Richard III, the eleventh of their twelve children, was born on 2 October 1452 in the keep, which was positioned on the motte that has survived. There was no expectation that he would one day become of King of England. During October, Henry VI visited Fotheringhay Castle on his progress to Peterborough and would have encountered the newborn baby.

Richard spent the first seven of his formative years at Fotheringhay Castle without his parents. A year after his birth, his father, York, was appointed Protector of the Realm after Henry VI had succumbed to illness and was unable to rule. After the Battle of St Albans, his father would move between his homes at Ludlow, Sandal and Fotheringhay. Despite being born into a large family, Richard did not share his childhood with some of his siblings and did not get the opportunity to know them. His elder brothers, Edward and Edmund, lived at Ludlow Castle. Anne and Elizabeth were educated in the houses of noblemen. The siblings nearest his age were Margaret, aged 6, and George, aged 3, whom he was able to play with within Fotheringhay Castle. Margaret would become a maternal figure in Richard's life.

When Queen Margaret was mobilising an army to counter the Yorkist claim to the throne during 1459, York considered that it was not safe for his children, Richard, George and Margaret, to stay at Fotheringhay Castle and moved them to Ludlow Castle, where they would be more secure.

Masonry from Fotheringhay Castle and the motte from where there are panoramic views of the surrounding countryside and the River Nene, which flows between fields towards the Wash. (Author's collection)

All that remains of Fotheringhay Castle are the earthworks of the castle motte and ditches as well as a block of limestone masonry enclosed by railings. A plaque commemorates the birthplace of Richard III and another is dedicated to Mary Queen of Scots, who was imprisoned at Fotheringhay Castle from 1586 until her execution in the Great Hall on 8 February 1587. The castle fell into ruins after the Tudor period.

10
Statue of Margaret of Anjou, Angers

Margaret of Anjou was the most ruthless and redoubtable woman in English history.

After the deaths of Cardinal Henry Beaufort and Humphrey, Duke of Gloucester, Queen Margaret played a prominent role in English politics. She insisted that she be kept informed on the governing of the country, including its economy, military and foreign policies. After Suffolk's death in 1450, Margaret relied upon Somerset, the King's advisor, who did not act unless he had her authority. Any decree signed by Henry VI had to be supported by an authorised letter from the queen. She also requested to see reports of dissenters and any dissension within the kingdom.

The placid nature of Henry VI made it easy for Queen Margaret to dominate him and influence national policy. She would support policies that favoured French interests that would conflict with Richard, 3rd Duke of York, who supported the occupation of France. Her despising of York would transform into a toxic obsession as she attempted to thwart challenges from him and later from his son, Edward, to her husband's throne. Allying herself with extremist elements in court that opposed York, the politically perceptive Margaret became a formidable and determined opponent.

Margaret and Henry VI were completely unsuited with regard to their personalities. He was regarded as weak, but Margaret was a strong, decisive character who would loyally champion his right to reign, thus becoming the dominant partner in their marriage. Margaret would become the power behind the docile Henry VI's throne. His lack of engagement as king left a power vacuum, which she filled in matters of state. Margaret displayed her political acumen as she instigated alliances, engaged in plotting and raised armies on behalf of her husband. Margaret favoured the Beaufort family; after all, Cardinal Henry Beaufort had supported her marriage to Henry VI and he had become a personal friend. She believed that she was helping her husband's position, but by her allegiance to this family she was causing further friction and division among opposing families.

Statue of Margaret of Anjou in Angers. (Courtesy of Chabe01; via Wikimedia Commons)

11
Statue of Henry VI

Henry VI suffered a mental and physical breakdown.

Henry was a strong advocate for education. In 1440, he established the King's College of our Lady of Eton, now known as Eton College. This bronze statue that stands at Eton College depicts Henry VI in mid-life prior to becoming incapacitated by ill health during 1453.

On 17 July 1453, the last battle of the Hundred Years' War was fought at Castillon in Gascony, resulting in an English defeat. This was humiliating for the king and damaged the nation's pride and confidence, because for the exception of Calais, all the lands that Henry VI inherited from his father, Henry V, in France had been lost during his reign. The shock of this news had a detrimental impact upon the king's health and when he was residing at his hunting lodge at Clarendon during August 1453, he became incapacitated, unable to move or communicate. He had been stricken by a condition that left him mentally and physically paralysed. His grandfather, Charles VI of France, had also suffered a similar condition. Physicians administered various medications to help the king recover, but to no avail. For eighteen months Henry VI would be without sense and unable to rise from a chair without assistance. Henry did not have an heir, and there was concern for who would reign over England while the king was unable to rule. The king's illness awakened the rivalries and contentions for the throne of England between the houses of York and Lancaster. Henry's wife, Queen Margaret, who was aged 23 and seven months pregnant, was left to make decisions on behalf of her husband.

Statue of Henry VI at Eton College. (Courtesy of Kazimierz Mendlik; via Wikimedia Commons)

12

Windsor Castle

Henry VI convalesced at Windsor Castle.

Windsor Castle played a prominent role during the Wars of the Roses because it was the birthplace of Henry VI, it was used as place of refuge when he became ill, it was used as a country residence by Edward IV and it served briefly as a prison for Queen Margaret. St George's Chapel would eventually become the place of burial for Henry VI and Edward IV.

Henry VI was born at Windsor Castle on 6 December 1421 and remained there until 13 November 1423, when his mother Catherine brought him to London to open Parliament. The royal abode at Windsor Castle was not maintained during the reign of Henry VI, with minimal repairs carried out and traditions such as the Garter feasts being abandoned.

In 1453, the castle served as a sanctuary for Henry VI during his breakdown when he was incapable of performing his royal duties. Margaret feared that if he resided at the Palace of Westminster, it would be impossible to conceal his condition from court and that risked York seizing power, so she decided that Henry VI should live at Windsor. His condition was so severe, he was unable to speak and unaware of what was occurring around him. This lack of awareness was so severe that he was oblivious to the fact that Margaret had given birth to their son Edward at the Palace of Westminster on 13 October 1453. The Yorkist elements of the population received the news of the birth with disdain, questioning how Henry could be the natural son of Henry VI after eight years of marriage to Margaret when no child was conceived. Henry VI appeared confused and was unable to bless and acknowledge his son as heir to the throne when Humphrey Stafford, 1st Duke of Buckingham, brought the baby to Windsor Castle to present him to the king.

Although the birth of an heir had strengthened Queen Margaret's position, without acknowledgment from the king, their position was not secure. The birth of an heir would diminish the claim of the House of York to the throne. At St Paul's Cross in London, Richard Neville, 16th Earl of Warwick, tried to spread the incorrect rumour that the young prince was the product of an adulterous relationship, which would have forfeited his right to the throne.

Aerial view of Windsor Castle. (EQRoy/Shutterstock)

Margaret and Buckingham returned to Windsor Castle on 19 January 1454 with the prince, who was known as Edward of Westminster, hoping that Henry VI would recognise his son, but to no avail. According to Abbott John Whethamstede, the king 'was so lacking in understanding and memory and so incapable that he was neither able to walk upon his feet nor to lift up his head, nor to move himself from the place he was seated'.[7]

After defeating the Lancastrians in 1461, Edward IV would frequently stay at Windsor Castle, where he would hunt in nearby woods and was responsible for renovating the castle. After Queen Margaret had landed at Weymouth in 1471, Edward used Windsor Castle as a rallying point to assemble his army. On 23 April 1471, while celebrating the Feast of St George at Windsor Castle, he was informed that Queen Margaret was heading for Wales and during the next day he led his army from the castle to confront her. After her capture at Tewkesbury and the death of Henry VI, Queen Margaret was briefly imprisoned at Windsor Castle.

---

7. Whethamstede, Reg. Mon. St. Albani (Rolls Ser.), p.163.

13

Engraving depicting Westminster

Richard, 3rd Duke of York, proclaimed Protector of England.

The Palace of Westminster was the principal royal residence and official centre of government during the medieval period, where Parliament had met since the thirteenth century. This engraving shows Westminster Abbey, the Parliament House and the Palace of Westminster, including Westminster Hall, which along with the Jewel House are the only remnants of the medieval palace.

Given that Henry VI was incapacitated at Windsor Castle, Parliament did not savour the prospect of another minor becoming sovereign and debated the prospect of a regency during early 1454. On 27 March, peers in the Houses of Parliament proclaimed York as protector to govern England, while the King was indisposed.

So long as Henry VI remained childless, York would be regarded as heir to the throne, albeit unofficially, because he was a direct descendent of Lionel, Duke of Clarence, through his mother's lineage and Edmund of Langley, 1st Duke of York, through his father's line. The birth of Prince Edward on 13 October 1453 meant that York was no longer heir to the throne. York continued to regard Edmund Beaufort, 2nd Duke of Somerset, who served as Chief of the King's Ministers, as a bad influence upon Henry VI. He blamed his military failures for the loss of English-occupied land in France and imprisoned him in the Tower of London. While protector, York was appointed Captain of Calais, which meant that he was responsible for the defence of England's last bastion in France.

When Henry VI rallied from his infirmity at Windsor Castle and recognised his son during December 1454, he was reinstated as sovereign. York was compelled to surrender his position as Lord Protector as his role was no longer required. The king also dismissed York as Captain of Calais and replaced him with Somerset, whom he released from the Tower of London on 7 February 1455.

Queen Margaret had much influence over her husband, but when he became incapacitated she instigated the transfer of the court and government from Westminster in London to the Midlands in places such as Coventry, Leicester and Kenilworth, where there was strong Lancastrian support that she could mobilise. Together with Somerset, Queen Margaret planned a special council meeting of nobles to meet in Leicester on 21 May 1455 to discuss the security

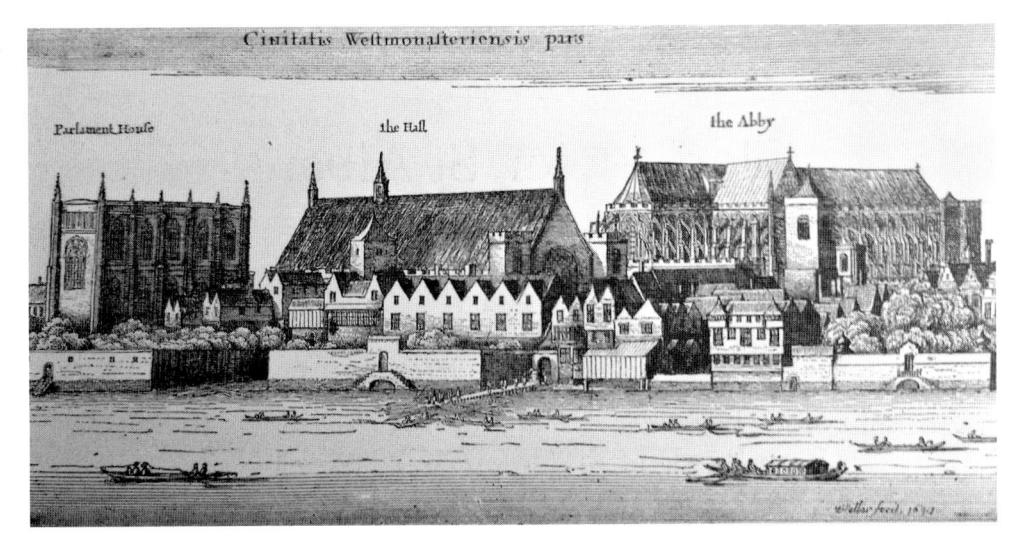

Westminster from an engraving by Wenceslaus Hollar featuring, from left to right, Parliament House, Westminster Hall and Westminster Abbey. (Author's collection)

of Henry VI. This meeting excluded York, but he was summoned to the city alone without his soldiers. York feared that at this meeting, Somerset would bring charges against him as a traitor. Fearing that his life was in immediate danger, York was determined to depose Somerset and remove his influence from the king once and for all, then restore his own position on the council. Supported by his brother-in-law, Richard Neville, 5th Earl of Salisbury, and his son Richard Neville, 16th Earl of Warwick, who had disagreements with Somerset, York mobilised an army for their own protection and led the force to intercept Henry VI on his journey between London and Leicester. The two armies would clash at St Albans.

14

Clocktower, St Albans

The bell Gabriel was sounded from this clocktower before the First Battle of St Albans on 22 May 1455.

This bell not only alerted the Lancastrians defending St Albans that the Yorkist army was approaching the town, it also heralded the first battle of the Wars of the Roses. This particular confrontation was not a battle for the crown, because at that time York remained loyal to Henry VI and his only intention was to remove his advisor, Edmund Beaufort, 2nd Duke of Somerset. It was therefore not a direct challenge to Henry VI, but a battle for who would be the king's chief advisor.

The clocktower has stood in St Albans for 600 years. In 1403, the townspeople commissioned Thomas Wolvey, a former Royal Mason, to build this clocktower in the marketplace. There was tension between the abbot of St Albans and traders, who wanted to have a belfry in which they could control the hours of business and trading. By having their own belfry, they could decide the hours in which they worked, independent of the church. It is the only town belfry that has existed from medieval times in England. Completed in 1405, it was built 19.5m (64 ft) high. It towered over the houses in the town and was an ideal observation position. The walls were built using flint rubble in lime mortar and measured 4ft thick to withstand the reverberations of the bell that was installed on the fourth floor. The clocktower is a symbol of the traders' resistance against the power of the Abbot of St Albans.

The original bell, named Gabriel, after the archangel, is still in place. It was cast in Aldgate, London, by William Robert Burford, who was active between 1371 and 1418. The bell weighs 1 ton and measures 1.2m (46 inches) in diameter. The following rhyme is inscribed in Latin, 'From Heaven I came, Gabriel my name'. During medieval times, the bell pealed to ring the Angelus at 4 am to awaken the people in the town and the curfew between 8 pm and 9 pm.

During the early morning of 22 May 1455, the Lancastrian army of Henry VI arrived at St Albans, supported by Thomas Clifford, 8th Baron Clifford; Edmund Beaufort, 2nd Duke of Somerset; and Humphrey Stafford, 1st Duke of Buckingham; with his eldest son, Humphrey Stafford, Earl of Stafford; Henry Percy, 2nd Earl of Northumberland; and James Butler, 1st Earl of Wiltshire. The Lancastrians approached the town from the south-west, moving up Holywell Hill and St Peter's Street. The clocktower provided a platform for Lancastrian

The Clocktower at St Albans was held by the Lancastrians during the First Battle of St Albans in 1455. Six years later Yorkist archers were positioned around its base, where they repelled a Lancastrian assault during the Second Battle of St Albans on 17 February 1461. (Author's collection)

The bell Gabriel was used to sound the alarm to the Lancastrian Army as the Yorkists approached on 22 May 1455. The parapet and spirelet were added to the structure during the Victorian era. Gabriel was last rung to acknowledge the funeral of Queen Victoria in 1901. (Author's collection)

observers to view all the approaches to the town. As soldiers belonging to the Yorkist army led by Richard, 3rd Duke of York; Richard Neville, 5th Earl of Salisbury; and Richard Neville, 16th Earl of Warwick; were approaching St Albans from the east from Ware, after marching from Sandal Castle in Yorkshire, Gabriel, the bell in St Albans Clocktower was sounded to raise the alert.

There are various sources that give different numbers for the strength of the Lancastrian and Yorkist armies that fought at the First Battle of St Albans. Some sources cite as many as 300,000 soldiers participated, which is an exaggeration. The Paston Letters confirmed a realistic number comprising 3,000 Lancastrian soldiers against 5,000 Yorkists.[8]

As soon as Somerset learned that the Yorkist army was approaching St Albans, he convinced Henry VI that York was attempting to usurp his throne, so that the king sided with Somerset. As soon as Somerset received intelligence that the Lancastrians were outnumbered by Yorkist forces, he decided to wait at St Albans for reinforcements instead of running the risk of being routed in exposed countryside on the journey to London.

---

8. Gairdner, James, *The Paston Letters 1422–1509 A.D. Volume One* (Public Records Office, London, 1872), p.332.

15

Map of St Albans in 1455

During the fifteenth century, St Albans was a small town that consisted of one principal thoroughfare, named St Peter's Street. The city did not have walls, so the roads that approached St Albans were barricaded. The marketplace was at the epicentre, with the clocktower. Another road branched north-eastwards to the north of St Albans Cathedral. The Lancastrians were positioned close to this clocktower and a contingent of men were prepared to defend the town from the clocktower eastwards into the marketplace and St Peter's Street.

At 7.00 am on 22 May 1455, the Yorkist forces arrived and assembled at Key Fields, which was south of the Tonman Ditch, a thirteenth-century excavation that stretched along the eastern perimeter of St Albans. It had a raised earth bank, which the Lancastrians utilised as a line of defence to oppose the advancing Yorkists. Forces belonging to Somerset and Northumberland were positioned behind the ditch on the left flank, with Clifford on the right flank.

Here the Yorkists waited for three hours. Once Henry VI became aware of the Yorkist army's presence, he sent Humphrey Stafford, 1st Duke of Buckingham, to Key Field to seek their intentions and with a message appealing for them to keep the peace. York, Salisbury and his son, Warwick, affirmed their allegiance, assuring Buckingham that they remained the king's faithful subjects and liegemen, but they requested that Henry VI surrender Somerset to their custody. The three Yorkist noblemen asserted that 'Heaven knoweth than our intent is rightful and true … Wherefore, gracious Lord, please your high Majesty to deliver such as we whole accuse … and we will now not cease for noon such promise, sure no other, till we have him which deserved death, or else we die therefore.'[9]

Henry VI refused to deliver Somerset to the Yorkists and, uncharacteristically belligerent, he gave the following response:

> I, King Harry, charge and command that no manner of person, of what degree, or state, or condition that ever he be, abide not, but void the field and not be so hardy as to make any resistance against me in mine own realm; for I shall know what traitor be so bold to

---

9. Gairdner, *The Paston Letters, Vol.1.*, op. cit., p.328.

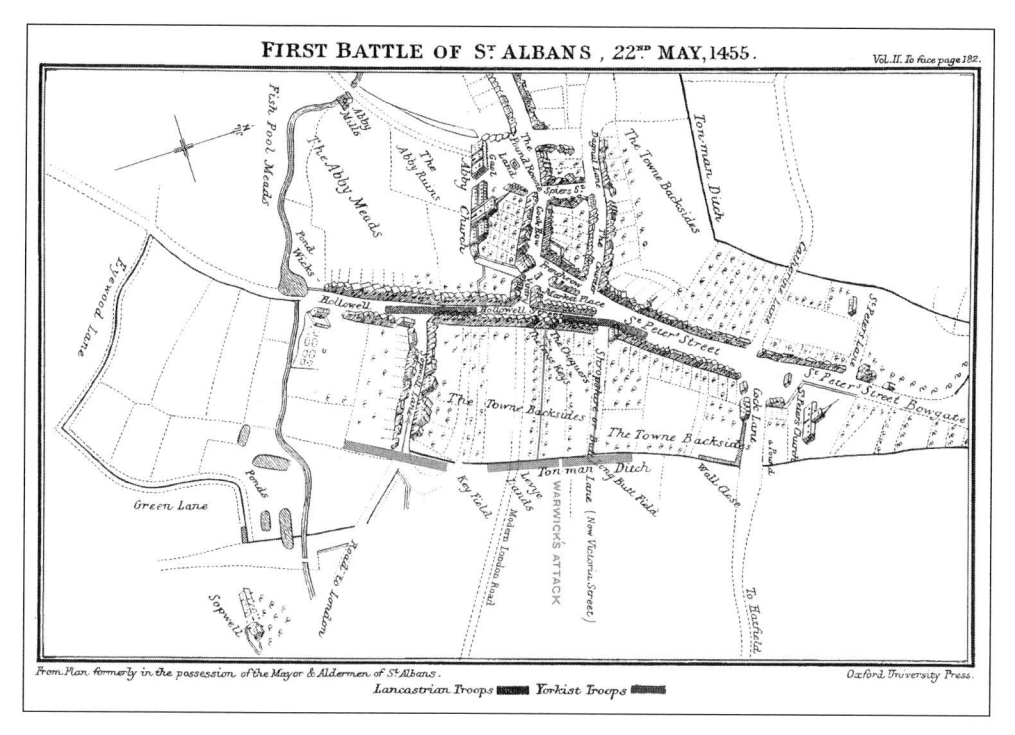

Map of St Albans as it would have appeared during May 1455. (Author's collection)

raise a people in mine own land, where through I am in great disease and heaviness. And by the faith that I owe St. Edward and to the Crown of England, I shall destroy them every mother's son; and they shall be hanged and drawn and quartered that may be taken afterward, of them to have example to all such traitors to beware to make any such rising of people within my land, and so traitorly to abide their King and governor. And for a conclusion, rather than they shall have any Lord here with me at this time, I shall this day, for their sake and in this quarrel, myself live or die.[10]

On receiving the king's response, York decided to attack St Albans and capture Somerset by force. The assault began between 11.00 am and midday. Warwick led the central column from Tonman Ditch, across a bank and through fields towards the town, but was blocked by the Lancastrians. His forces resorted to advancing through gardens of the houses in order to access the town and into Hollowell Lane. York initially tried to enter St Albans using Sopwell Lane (now Victoria Street) into St Peter's Street, but could not break through the barricades defended by Somerset's soldiers.

---

10. Ibid., p.328.

16

Plaque commemorating Edmund Beaufort, 2nd Duke of Somerset

Chief advisor to Henry VI was killed on this site during the First Battle of St Albans.

At the junction of Victoria Street and St Peter's Street there is plaque positioned on the wall of the Skipton Building Society that states this was where the Castle Inn was located and where Somerset was slain. Just north from this junction is the marketplace where Henry VI raised his standard.

The Castle Inn was Somerset's command post. Soldiers commanded by Henry VI held a line that stretched from the marketplace, along St Peter's Street, behind the building that houses the St Albans Museum up to the clocktower. When York received the message of the king's refusal to hand over Somerset to his forces, the First Battle of St Albans began. An unidentified chronicler, writing before 1471, wrote that 'when the Duke of York and the Earls heard this answer, though the town were strongly barred and arrayed for defence, they and their people broke down violently houses and pales on the east side of the town, and entered in to Saint Peters Street slaying all that withstood them'.[11]

Yorkist soldiers belonging to York broke through the Tonman Ditch and advanced from the south-east along Victoria Street, charging up the slope towards the Castle Inn, where the plaque is situated. Edward Hall's chronicle stated that, 'then came the duke of Somerset, and all the other lords with the King's power, which fought a sore and a cruel battle, in which many a tall man lost his life'.[12]

Looking in a south-westerly direction towards Chequer Street from the junction where the plaque is situated, Warwick's forces entered St Albans where the next set of traffic lights are positioned at the next junction. Trumpets were sounded amidst the cries of 'A Warwick! A Warwick! A Warwick!'[13] and very soon the Yorkists had entered St Albans. Close-quarter

---

11. Davies, Rev., John. Ed., *An English Chronicle of the Reigns of Richard II, Henry IV, Henry V and Henry VI written before 1471* (Camden Society, 1856), p.71.

12. Hall, Edward, *Hall's Chronicle: Henry IV to Henry VIII* (First Published 1548, J. Johnson, London, 1809), p.232.

13. Gairdner, *The Paston Letters, Vol.1.*, op. cit., p.328.

Site of the Castle Inn where Edmund Beaufort, Duke of Somerset, was killed during the Battle of St Albans in 1455. (Author's collection)

fighting took place in the houses and narrow alleyways north of Chequer Street, and the Yorkists eventually fought their way into St Peter's Street and the marketplace. Abbot John Whethamstede witnessed the battle and wrote that 'so strongly were they opposed, here you saw one fall with his brains dashed out, there another with a broken arm, a third with a cut throat, and a fourth with a pierced chest and the whole street was full of dead corpses'.[14]

Henry VI had left the confines of St Albans Abbey with Somerset to assess the progress of the battle at St Peter's Street, where the Standard was placed in the marketplace. It was the first time that the king, aged 33, had experienced battle. Longbow men belonging to Warwick shot a flight of arrows at this position. Henry VI was slightly injured with a flesh wound during the battle. An anonymous chronicler recorded that, 'the King that stood under his banner was hurt in the neck with an arrow'.[15]

Other noblemen were struck by the arrows shot by Yorkist archers. Humphrey Stafford, 1st Duke of Buckingham, was wounded by an arrow in the face, while his son, Sir Henry Stafford, sustained a wound in the hand. As the fighting intensified, the Lancastrian defence

---

14. Whethamstede, op. cit., p.168.

15. Davies, op. cit., p.71.

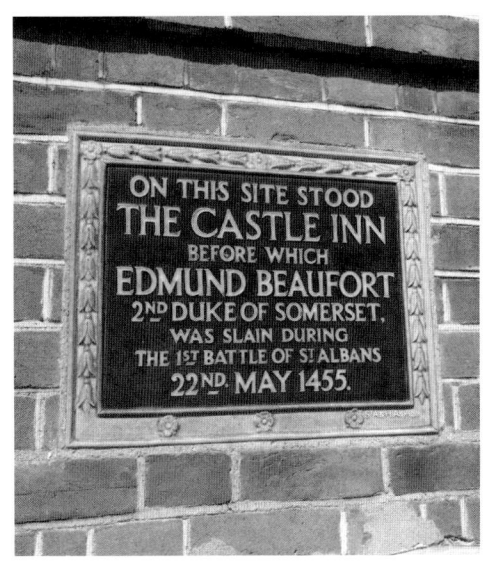

Plaque denoting site where Somerset was slain. (Author's collection)

began to collapse. Sir Philip Wentworth lowered the Royal Standard and fled the town. This resulted in a reduction in morale and confidence. Wentworth was soon followed by James Butler, 1st Earl of Wiltshire, and his 500 men, together with members of the King's Household. Wiltshire had escaped the town disguised as a monk[16] and would be renowned as a coward for abandoning his men at the Battles of Mortimer's Cross and Towton. As Clifford's soldiers were being overwhelmed by Warwick's men, Somerset rushed forward to stop them from entering the marketplace. Somerset's son, Henry Beaufort, aged 19, fought alongside his father until he was severely wounded and evacuated from the town on a cart. At the Castle Inn, Somerset was killed alongside Henry Percy, 2nd Earl of Northumberland, and Thomas, 8th Baron Clifford. Hall recorded that 'there died under the sign of the Castle, Edmund, Duke of Somerset, who long before was warned to eschew all castles'.[17]

Somerset had heard a prophecy from a fortune teller that he should not go under a castle for fearful consequences, and for that reason he refused the king's invitations to visit him at Windsor Castle. At St Albans he was fighting beneath the sign to the Castle Inn and when he realised that the prophecy was becoming reality, Somerset lost his mind and was killed. William Shakespeare mentioned the Castle Inn in his play Henry VI, Part 2, when Richard, Duke of York said:

So, lie thou there –
For, underneath an alehouse' paltry sign,
The Castle in Saint Albans, Somerset
Hath made the wizard famous in death.

At the point when Somerset was bludgeoned to death the battle ceased after thirty minutes of fighting. The Paston Letters reported that 120 men were killed in the battle. 'There was at most slain vi score.'[18] Corpses lay at the head of every street in St Albans.

---

16. Jones, Dan, *The Hollow Crown* (Faber & Faber, London, 2014), p.150.

17. Hall, op. cit., p.233.

18. Ramsay, Sir James, *Lancaster & York* (Clarendon Press, Oxford, 1892), p.183.

17

St Albans Cathedral and Abbey Gatehouse

St Albans Cathedral and the gatehouse are all that remains of the monastery that existed during the Wars of the Roses.

During the days of the Wars of the Roses it was known as St Albans Abbey, but a large proportion of the monastic buildings that were familiar to Henry VI were destroyed during the Dissolution in 1539. The abbey was renovated and it became a cathedral when St Albans received its city charter in 1877.

It was at St Albans Abbey that Henry VI briefly stopped during his journey from London to Leicester during the early hours of 22 May 1455. As the Yorkist army descended upon St Peter's Street and the marketplace, the king left the confines of the abbey to monitor the progress of the fighting in the marketplace. After Buckingham had sustained an arrow wound to his face, he was brought to the sanctuary of St Albans Abbey.

When the Lancastrian defence was breached and its leaders were wounded, killed or fled, Henry VI sought refuge in a tanner's shop, where his neck wound was tended. It was here that he was found by York, Warwick and Salisbury, who 'on their knees besought him of grace and forgiveness'[19] and assured him that he would not come to harm. The deposition of Somerset was the objective and they did not want to give the impression that the confrontation at St Albans, often regarded as a skirmish, was a treasonous act of usurpation. It was never their intention to harm the king or supplant him from his throne. Treating their sovereign with the utmost respect and courtesy, York, the conqueror, declared his loyalty and willingness to obey him. He also discussed his fear that if he and his supporters had gone to Leicester, they would have been arrested as traitors, potentially executed and all their estates and wealth forfeited to the Crown. Henry VI accepted their justification and replied, 'Stop the pursuit and slaughter, and I will do whatever you will.'[20]

At that point York ordered the cessation of hostilities and the captive Henry VI was brought to St Albans Abbey, where at the shrine of St Alban, York, Warwick and Salisbury asked Henry VI to appoint them as his advisors. It was recorded that 'during the battle the duke of

---

19. Gairdner, *The Paston Letters, Vol.1.*, op. cit., p.328.

20. Edgar, J.G., *The Wars of the Roses* (Published London, 1870), pp.47–8.

St Albans Cathedral from the roof of the clocktower. (Author's collection)

York and the other lords had the king into the abbey and there kept him unhurt and there the king granted to be ruled by them'.[21] Henry VI had been defeated and had no choice but to comply with their request. York had established a triumvirate with Warwick and Salisbury, seizing power from Henry VI and rendering him king only in name.

York also found a distressed Abbot Whethamstede inside the abbey, who was concerned that Yorkist soldiers were pillaging the town and was fearful that they would eventually start plundering the abbey. He was also distressed that the remains of those killed were left on the streets, including the Lancastrian noblemen, Somerset, Northumberland and Clifford. Abbot Whethamstede protested to York about this situation and requested permission to bring these individuals and the bodies of forty-seven other men into St Albans Abbey. York agreed and they were buried together in the Lady Chapel of St Albans Abbey in a line according to their birth and rank, however their tombs have been lost over the centuries. It was at St Albans Abbey that York and Henry VI stayed during the evening after the battle, where they prayed with Abbot Whethamstede at the Shrine of St Alban, and on the next morning they travelled to London.

---

21. Fenley, Ralph, *Six Town Chronicles* (Clarendon Press, Oxford, 1911), p.158.

Gatehouse to St Albans Abbey. (Author's collection)

The First Battle of St Albans achieved York's ultimate aim, which was the removal of Somerset. Henry VI pardoned all those who supported the rebels. York was appointed Constable of England and became the king's chief advisor and Somerset's successor. Warwick, who had distinguished himself during this battle and would later become known as Warwick the Kingmaker, was appointed Captain of Calais. After the battle, London was no longer regarded as a safe place for Henry VI, so the royal court and parliament were temporarily moved to Coventry. As Henry VI drifted into psychosis in November 1455, potentially because of the loss of Somerset and the defeat at St Albans, York was appointed as Protector for three further months, where he attempted to initiate policies that would reign in the nation's debt and reform government. Some factions in parliament were suspicious of York's motives and were not supportive.

In February 1456, supporters of Henry VI rallied and revoked York's appointment as Protector, although he was invited to remain on the council. After losing control of the court and government, York returned to Ireland in 1456. Although the situation was fragile, the Yorkist victory at St Albans brought peace to England for the next four years, but the tensions remained and the battle had created a blood feud. York, Warwick and Salisbury tried to avert that scenario by trying to make amends by sponsoring a chantry at St Albans Abbey dedicated to those on all sides who died during the first battle. York donated 5,000 marks to Somerset's widow and family, while he compensated 1,000 marks to the Clifford family. These hollow gestures for the deaths of Edmund Beaufort, 2nd Duke of Somerset, and Henry Percy, 2nd Earl of Northumberland, left their sons, who had also fought at St Albans, with a determination to avenge the loss of their fathers.

St Albans Abbey had several further connections with the Wars of the Roses. As previously mentioned, Humphrey, Duke of Gloucester, uncle to Henry VI, was buried here in 1447.

Above left: The Shrine of St Alban. Henry VI agreed to appoint York, Warwick and Salisbury as his advisors after the first battle of St Albans. (Author's collection)

Above right: The Lady Chapel, St Albans Cathedral, where casualties from the first battle were buried. (Author's collection)

Edward IV passed through the town on his journey from London to Towton in 1461. During 1483, Edward V stayed one night at St Albans Abbey with his uncle, Richard, Duke of Gloucester, on his ill-fated journey from Stony Stratford to the Tower of London. His sister, Elizabeth of York, would visit St Albans Abbey with Henry VII on their journey to London for the coronation of Elizabeth during November 1487.

18

Pembroke Castle

Birthplace of Henry Tudor, Henry VII.

Work to build Pembroke Castle began in 1066 after the Norman conquest, as a defence against Welsh insurgents. William Marshal, 1st Earl of Pembroke, began transforming the castle into a strong stone bastion in 1189 and it took thirty years to build the structure that we see today. It is the only castle in Britain to be constructed over a natural cave, known as the Wogan Cavern.

Henry VI granted Pembroke Castle and the Earldom of Pembroke to Jasper Tudor in 1452. Jasper and his brother, Edmund, were stepbrothers of Henry VI, from Catherine de Valois, his mother's second marriage to Owen Tudor.

Statue of Henry VII and Pembroke Castle, his birthplace. (Courtesy of Phillip Halling; www.geograph.org.uk)

On 28 January 1457, Henry Tudor, the future King Henry VII, was born at Pembroke Castle within a tower overlooking Westgate. The tower where it is believed that he was born was a guard chamber that formed part of the outer ward and is now known as Henry VII Tower and regarded as the birthplace of the Tudor dynasty. Henry's mother, Lady Margaret Beaufort, was widowed when her husband, Edmund Tudor, 1st Earl of Richmond, died from bubonic plague on 3 November 1456 while being held captive by Yorkist forces at Carmarthen Castle. His brother, Jasper Tudor, Earl of Pembroke, took responsibility for the pregnant Margaret, who was aged between 12 and 14 years old. Henry Tudor would live during the early part of his childhood at Pembroke Castle with his mother and uncle Jasper.

The castle was seized by Yorkist forces in 1461. Henry's guardianship was passed to the Yorkist William Herbert, along with the earldom of Pembrokeshire and Pembroke Castle. Lady Margaret Beaufort remarried Sir Henry Stafford and later Thomas Stanley, 1st Earl of Derby. She would become a determined and formidable force in ensuring that her son, Henry, ascended the English throne.

19

The ragged staff emblem

The heraldic emblem of the Earls of Warwick, first used by the Beauchamp family from 1268 and adopted by Richard Neville, the 16th Earl of Warwick, which was worn by his followers.

Richard Neville, known as Warwick the Kingmaker, was a valiant soldier and formidable power broker during the Wars of the Roses. He was confident, charismatic and possessed the gravitas to rouse the populace to his side. Driven by ambition and self-interest, he was able to manipulate and influence situations that would benefit himself and his family.

Richard Neville was the eldest son of Richard Neville, 5th Earl of Salisbury, and became the 16th Earl of Warwick through his marriage to Anne Beauchamp, 15th Countess of Warwick. Through this marriage and his own family inheritance he became England's most affluent landowner and powerful nobleman. His support was pivotal in influencing who would be sovereign during the Wars of the Roses, which earned him the name of 'Kingmaker'. Warwick's aunt, Cecily, had married Richard, Duke of York, but his support of York during the Wars of the Roses was not due to family loyalty, but driven by the Nevilles' rivalry with the Percy family and control of Northumberland and Westmoreland. This had escalated into a local civil war during 1453–54, with small battles being fought at Stamford Bridge and Heworth in Yorkshire. The Percys were ardent supporters of the House of Lancaster, which gave Warwick and the Nevilles an additional incentive to align themselves with the Yorks. Warwick also shared resentment with York towards Somerset through land disputes in the Welsh Marches. Warwick demonstrated tremendous arrogance when he defied inheritance laws to seize the entire lordship of Glamorgan using force, despite Henry VI granting this land to Somerset. The allegiance between York and the Nevilles created a powerful alliance. When York became Protector during 1453, Warwick was appointed Lord Chancellor and joined the King's Council.

In 1456 Warwick was appointed Captain of Calais and when the Lancastrians took control of Parliament he retained control of Calais, refusing to surrender the garrison town to Queen Margaret. During the following four years he had the financial means to pay the garrison soldiers from his own assets. He continued to defend the Calais garrison from French attempts to seize the port, and even went on the offensive. It was Warwick who was fighting the Yorkist cause while in Calais between 1456 to 1460. Queen Margaret sent Henry Beaufort, 3rd Duke of Somerset (whose father had died at the First Battle of St Albans), to capture the Calais garrison from Warwick from his base at Guisnes.

Warwick would continue to fight for the Yorkist cause at St Albans and Towton. His support in assisting Edward IV seize the throne was rewarded with the appointment of Constable of Dover Castle, Warden of the Cinque Ports and of the West and East Marches of Scotland. Warwick was also appointed Great Chamberlain of England. His relationship would deteriorate when Edward IV married Elizabeth Woodville in 1464.

Ragged staff emblem of Warwick. (Author's collection)

20

Audley's Cross, Blore Heath

The Yorkists defeated Queen Margaret's forces in Staffordshire.

Audley's Cross marks the spot where James Tuchet (sometimes written Touchet), 5th Baron Audley, was killed. He was aged 61, and the last time he had experienced battle was twenty-eight years earlier during the Hundred Years' War. It is believed that a cross was erected to mark where Audley was killed soon after the battle. The existing cross was repaired in 1765.

Margaret was not comfortable that Richard, Duke of York, served as her husband's chief councillor and posed a threat to her son's succession to the throne. In 1459 Margaret attempted to remove York's influence upon her husband's court by inviting all noblemen to attend a meeting in Coventry except for York, Warwick and his father, Salisbury. Margaret, aged 29, had gained strength and confidence, and was politically astute to engage a network of support from allies to fight for her husband's lawful right to govern and protect her son's inheritance. Determined and resolute, Margaret planned to conspire against them and charge them with acts of treason. Aware of this conspiracy, Warwick, who had recently landed in Sandwich, Kent, with elements from the Calais garrison, was now in London, and Salisbury planned to join forces to meet with York at Ludlow Castle. The conflict between the Houses of York and Lancaster would resume at Blore Heath in Staffordshire on 23 September 1459.

Salisbury, leading 5,000 Yorkist soldiers,[22] was marching from Middleham Castle to join his brother-in-law at Ludlow Castle. Margaret ordered Baron Audley to intercept Salisbury's men and that Thomas Stanley, 1st Earl of Derby, join the Lancastrian army. Stanley was the son-in-law of Salisbury and despite confirming that he would come forward, he did not fulfil that promise. As Audley passed through Shropshire and Cheshire, he mustered a force of 10,000 men and was able to manoeuvre his army in between Salisbury's and York's forces.[23]

---

22. Twemlow, Francis Randle, *The Battle of Blore Heath* (Whitehead Printers, Wolverhampton, 1912), p.1.

23. Ibid., p.1.

Above: Audley's Cross marks the spot where Lord Audley was killed at the Battle of Blore Heath. (Courtesy of Colin Park; via Wikimedia Commons)

Below: Plaque at the entrance to Blore Heath Farm, site of the Lancastrian camp in 1459. (Courtesy of John Lord; www.geograph.org.uk)

During the evening of 22 September 1459, Audley intercepted Salisbury's forces at Blore Heath, which is close to Market Drayton in Shropshire. Audley and the Lancastrians greatly outnumbered Salisbury's Yorkist army and was positioned north on the slope behind a stream, known as Hempmill Brook, which had steep banks. Salisbury did not expect the Lancastrians to cross the stream and launch an attack, so he ordered his men to set up camp for the night.

Instead of crossing the stream to attack the Lancastrians, Salisbury decided to use its steep banks to set a trap. During the following morning, 23 September, Salisbury ordered his archers to shoot arrows across the stream into Audley's camp and then pretend to retreat. Audley took the bait and gave orders for his soldiers to pursue the Yorkists across the stream. As soon as they reached the northern bank, Salisbury's men turned and attacked them before they ascended the bank. Two thousand Lancastrians were slain, including Audley, and prominent noblemen from Lancashire and Cheshire, including the heads of the Lancastrian families of Egerton, Legh, Molyneux and Venables.[24] The battle lasted for four hours and after the loss of these commanders, the Lancastrian army was broken and the battle lost. While the battle was being fought, the queen was residing with her son at Eccleshall Castle.

The victorious Salisbury was cautious because he was aware that a strong Lancastrian force that outnumbered his men could easily follow and rout them as they headed towards Ludlow. Therefore, Salisbury ordered his artillery to maintain a rearguard action, and left a friar to continue to fire the cannon to give the false impression that the Yorkists had encamped at Blore Heath, when in fact they were concealing their move to Ludlow during the night to join York.[25]

---

24. Edgar, J.G., op. cit., p.64.

25. Gairdner, James, *William Gregory's Chronicle of London* (Camden Society, 1876), p.204.

21
Ludlow Castle

The family home of the York Family in the Welsh Marches during the War of Roses.

Overlooking a gorge of the River Teme, Ludlow Castle was strongly fortified. The castle was built shortly after the Norman conquest in 1066 and Richard, 3rd Duke of York, inherited it during 1425, through his mother's lineage, the Mortimers, who expanded the castle when they acquired it in 1301. Edward, Earl of March (future Edward IV), spent his childhood at Ludlow Castle along with his brother, Edmund, Earl of Rutland.

Expecting Queen Margaret to challenge him militarily, York feared that Fotheringhay Castle was not a safe place for his younger children, Richard (future Richard III), George and Margaret, to live and summoned them to reside at Ludlow Castle during the spring 1459. It was here where they would meet and become acquainted with their elder brothers, Edward, aged 17, and Edmund, 16. The young Richard would see them practise the skills of wielding an axe and swordsmanship.

Ludlow Castle, the Yorkist stronghold in Wales. (Richard Hayman/Shutterstock)

On 25 September 1459, seven days before his seventh birthday, Richard first became exposed to war as he watched Richard Neville, 5th Earl of Salisbury, arrive at Ludlow Castle after his victory at Blore Heath and saw wounded soldiers transported on carts and the damage done to armour worn on the battlefield. In that month, York raised his standard and summoned his followers to Ludlow to protect his family and estates from Queen Margaret.

Warriors from all over England responded to York's battle cry and descended upon Ludlow Castle, including Salisbury's son, Warwick, who brought 600 soldiers from the Calais garrison commanded by Andrew Trollope. Anticipating a Lancastrian attack, York ordered the excavation of a defensive ditch on the other side of the River Teme from Ludlow. The sons of York would realise at Ludlow that they were living in a dangerous world where their lineage was under threat.

Ludlow Castle would later become the home of Edward, Prince of Wales (future Edward V). When he reached the age of 3, his father, Edward IV, established a household at the castle where he was cared for by his brother-in-law, Anthony Woodville, 2nd Earl of Rivers. It was here in 1483 that the Prince of Wales would learn of his father's death and that he had succeeded him as Edward V, King of England. He left Ludlow Castle for the last time on 4 May 1483 for London for his coronation. Henry VII and Elizabeth of York also used Ludlow Castle as the home for their son, Arthur, Prince of Wales. After Arthur married Catherine of Aragon, he became sick and died at Ludlow Castle on 2 April 1502.

22

Ludford Bridge

Ludford Bridge was constructed over the River Teme during the fifteenth century and restored in 1886.

During early October 1459 Henry VI and his loyalist supporters, numbering 30,000 men, were heading towards Ludlow. When he reached Worcester, the king received a petition from some Yorkist nobles declaring their loyalty and petitioned for peace.

Yorkist forces blocked the road approaching Ludlow by Ludlow Bridge on the southern bank of the River Teme, where barricades were built using stakes and carts, and a defensive ditch was dug that was filled with water from the river. It was from here, during the afternoon of 12 October 1459, that the banners of the royalists could be seen in the valley half a mile from their position by the river. The king's army was twice the size of the Yorkists and established a camp a mile from this bridge. Uncharacteristically, Henry VI

Ludford Bridge. (Courtesy of Roger Davies; www.geograph.org.uk)

was wearing full armour, but he did not want to provoke a civil war, so he offered a pardon to anyone who defected from the Yorkist cause, except for those who had fought against his forces at Blore Heath. Warwick had coerced Captain Andrew Trollope, the Master Porter of Calais, to accompany him to Ludlow on the pretence that they would not act against the king. During that evening, Trollope and the Calais garrison were unwilling to fight against the king. They crossed Ludford Bridge and defected to Henry VI's side. In the eyes of the Yorkists, this was a grievous act of betrayal, for Trollope was aware of the Yorkist defensive strategy. However, Trollope was a royalist who remained loyal to the Crown.

York, Salisbury and Warwick convened a meeting in the great hall of Ludlow Castle to consider their next move. Realising that they did not have sufficient support from Yorkist noblemen, that they were outnumbered by forces loyal to Henry VI, and that the plans to defend Ludlow were compromised, it was decided to disperse the Yorkist army and flee from Ludlow into Wales during the cover of night. York, with his son Edmund, Duke of Rutland, continued westward, requisitioned a ship and sailed for Ireland, where he was warmly received in Dublin, while Edward, Earl of March, with Salisbury accompanied by his cousin, Warwick, headed for the Devon coast, near Barnstaple. There, with the assistance of local nobleman Sir John Dynham, they bought a small ship and sailed to Guernsey, from where they then proceeded onto Calais. There they found that the garrison was held by Warwick's uncle, William Neville, 6th Baron Fauconberg. Dynham held the distinction of being a trusted councillor to Edward IV, Richard III and Henry VII.

During the following morning at Ludlow, the Yorkist troops who had been abandoned by their leaders knelt before Henry VI, who pardoned them. It was a bloodless battle, which resulted in Henry VI being the victor. York had not only deserted the men under his command, but his wife, Cecily Neville, Duchess of York, and their two young sons, George and Richard. They were captured in Ludlow and would not be freed until after the Battle of Northampton during July 1460. *Gregory's Chronicle* confirmed that after overindulging in the consumption of wine in the taverns, Henry's troops plundered the town and Ludlow Castle; that 'they robbed the town of bedding, clothes, and other stuff and defiled many women'.[26] The *English Chronicle* implied that Cecily Neville was raped, for it stated that 'the town of Ludlow was robbed to the bare walls and the noble duchess of York unmanly and cruelly entreated and spoiled'.[27]

York was attainted by Parliament, proclaimed a traitor and his property, including Ludlow Castle, forfeited to the Crown. After the ordeal at Ludlow, Henry VI behaved with decency towards Cecily, granting her an annual income to cover living expenses for her and her sons, as well as sending them to live under the custody of her sister, Anne, the Duchess of Buckingham, at Tonbridge Castle in Kent. As the Yorkist leaders fled the country for their lives as a consequence of the bloodless victory at Ludlow Bridge, Queen Margaret had restored the power to her husband's reign.

---

26. Gairdner, *Gregory's Chronicle*, op. cit., p.207.

27. Davies, op. cit., p.83.

23

Sandwich Quay

Embarkation and disembarkation port for nobles during the Wars of the Roses.

Sandwich is one of the original Cinque Ports, sheltered inland, approximately 10 miles north of Dover, which is connected to the English Channel by the River Stour. It was commonly used by merchants and by prominent figures during the medieval era.

Henry VI departed from Sandwich for Calais in 1430 on his journey to Paris for his coronation as King of France. Henry's inability to defend England's coastline left it vulnerable to attack and Sandwich was ransacked by a fleet of Norman and Breton ships commanded by Pierre de Brézé in 1457. The port would play a role in the Wars of the Roses during January 1460, when Henry VI sent Richard Woodville, Baron Rivers, with his son, Sir Anthony Woodville, to Sandwich to supress Yorkist supporters, which they captured together with Warwick's ship, which was berthed along the quay. Rivers, the father of Elizabeth, future wife of Edward IV, became the garrison commander at Sandwich. The plan was for the Lancastrians to assemble a fleet at Sandwich and send reinforcements to aid Henry Beaufort, 3rd Duke of Somerset (whose father had died at the First Battle of St Albans), in capturing the Calais garrison from Warwick from his base at Guisnes.

On 15 January 1460 Sir John Dynham led a detachment of Warwick's men disguised as merchantmen to raid Sandwich and they captured the fleet, including the recovery of Warwick's ships. Sir Anthony Woodville was intercepted in the town as well as his father, Richard, while they were asleep in bed in the friar's house. The people of Sandwich were Yorkist sympathisers and welcomed the raiders. Dynham was wounded during the raid, but he managed to bring principal ships with arms and munitions from Sandwich to Calais. The Woodvilles were also brought before Warwick and Edward, Earl of March, as prisoners and were verbally abused by them. It is ironic that four years later Richard Woodville would become Edward's father-in-law when he married his daughter, Elizabeth, and on his deathbed, Edward would entrust the custody of his son, Edward, Prince of Wales, to Sir Anthony Woodville, after his death.

Buoyed by the success of the raid upon Sandwich and confident that public opinion in England supported the Yorkist cause, Warwick went to Ireland to plan with York an assault

River Stour at Sandwich Quay, the point of disembarkation for Henry VI, Warwick and Edward, Earl of March, the future Edward IV. (Author's collection)

upon England from Ireland and a landing in the south-east of England using the ships and munitions that had been captured at Sandwich.

Warwick returned to Calais on 1 June 1460, and on 25 June Dynham led another assault upon Sandwich with Sir John Wenlock and William Neville, 6th Baron Fauconberg. They overwhelmed a Lancastrian force comprising 200 men and 200 archers, commanded by Sir Osbert Mundford, who were destined to join Somerset's campaign in France. Mundford's soldiers offered strong resistance and Dynham was wounded by a cannon shot to his leg. Mundford was captured and sent to Calais. He had previously served under Warwick in the garrison at Calais and was regarded as a traitor. He was beheaded at Rysbank Tower on 25 June 1460.

Fauconberg was left at Sandwich with a small Yorkist contingent to retain the port as a foothold and waited for the arrival of Warwick with a larger Yorkist force on the following day. On 26 June 1460, Richard Neville, 16th Earl of Warwick; Richard Neville, 5th Earl of Salisbury; and Edward, Earl of March; with 2,000 men, landed safely at Sandwich quay to launch a Yorkist campaign to challenge the House of Lancaster. They were welcomed by Archbishop Bourchier from Canterbury. It was from Sandwich that Warwick, Salisbury and March advanced upon London, mustering 30,000 followers[28] along their journey. According to Whethempstede, 40,000 men were behind the Yorkists and the gates of London were opened to them on 2 July 1460. Warwick and March continued north to confront the forces of Henry VI, who was holding his position in Coventry.

After the Yorkist victory at Towton in 1461, bonfires were lit at Sandwich and Dover to alert the garrison at Calais. Edward returned to Sandwich as king during his royal progress in August 1461. Ten years later, Richard, Duke of Gloucester, pursued William Neville's son, Thomas, the Bastard of Fauconberg, to Sandwich after his attempt to capture London during May 1471 had failed. It was along Sandwich Quay that Fauconberg surrendered his fleet and himself on the promise of a pardon.

---

28. Edgar, J.G., op. cit., p.65.

24

Eleanor Cross, Northampton

Yorkist victory at the Battle of Northampton.

The Eleanor Cross is all that survives from the battlefield at Northampton. It is situated at the south-eastern corner of the battlefield. This is one of twelve crosses that marked the stopping points along the route that brought the deceased Queen Eleanor, wife of Edward I, from Lincoln to London during 1290. The Yorkist army passed this Eleanor Cross during the morning of 10 July 1460.

Richard, 3rd Duke of York, was in Ireland. Henry VI and Margaret were in Coventry as Warwick and Edward, Earl of March, entered London. Margaret loaned money from the clergy and sought troops from the Beaufort, Beaumont, Percy, Stafford and Talbert families, who were loyal to the Lancastrian cause. Henry VI left Margaret and their son at Coventry and led the royalist troops to the southern bank of the River Nene, south of Northampton. The Yorkist army had superior numbers amounting to 20,000 soldiers, while Henry VI could muster 12,000 men. The Lancastrian army strengthened its position using the high ground close to the bend in the river where it was strongly protected on three sides by the river and deep trenches that were excavated on their front, fortified with piles and stakes. It was also supported by artillery.

By 7.00 am the Yorkists attacked the Lancastrian camp as it rained. Warwick charged on the field on horseback, wearing full armour, while March followed behind bearing his father's standard. The Lancastrian artillery was rendered ineffective due to the inclement weather, stuck in the mud, and its line was in disarray when Sir Edmund Grey betrayed Henry VI and joined the Yorkist side, displaying Warwick's ragged staff emblem. Grey's soldiers helped Edward and his Yorkist soldiers to penetrate the Lancastrian defences and dispersed the Lancastrians in all directions. It was possible that Warwick was aware of Grey's intention to defect to the Yorkist side prior to the battle.

Within an hour, the Lancastrian forces had been routed by the Yorkists. The common soldier was spared in accordance with Warwick's orders, but noblemen such as John Beaumont, 1st Viscount Beaumont; Thomas Percy, 1st Baron Egrement; John Talbot, 2nd Earl of Shrewsbury; and Sir William Lucy were slain. Some combatants saw the battle as an opportunity to resolve domestic disputes. Local knight Sir William Lucy heard the sounds

The Eleanor Cross, Northampton. (Courtesy of Brookie at English Wikipedia; via Wikimedia Commons)

of war from his home and came onto the battlefield to support Henry VI. Captain John Stafford on the Yorkist side was conducting an illicit affair with Lucy's wife, saw Sir William, whom he despised, and killed him with an axe. Stafford married Lady Lucy shortly after the battle.[29]

There were approximately 300 killed during the battle and many were drowned as they tried to retreat across the River Nene. Humphrey Stafford, 1st Duke of Buckingham, who commanded the royal army and was the king's guard, was killed while standing by the king's tent. Henry VI played no active role in the fighting and made no attempt to flee the battlefield after the Lancastrian defeat. He was found by Warwick and March sitting alone within his tent, where they bent their knees in respect and consoled him. They assured the king that they were loyal and their grievance was against his advisers. Henry VI was once again in Yorkist custody and was taken to Northampton, where on the following day, 11 July, the king and the Yorkist lords attended mass before riding to London. Queen Margaret and Prince Edward, who were at Eccleshall Castle in Staffordshire, fled in the direction of Wales.

---

29. Gairdner, *Gregory's Chronicle*, op. cit., p.207.

25

The Tower of London

Lancastrian soldiers defended the fortress against Yorkist attack.

The Tower of London features prominently in the story of the Wars of the Roses. It was a royal residence, monarchs stayed within its walls before their coronations, it was a prison, and it was a place where two kings – Henry VI and Edward V – died under mysterious circumstances. A royal menagerie was established at the Tower of the London during the reign of Edward IV, where his marmoset and three lions were kept together with bears and a dromedary (a camel) that was owned by his brother, George, Duke of Clarence. This segment focuses upon the period when the Yorkist army besieged the Tower of London in 1460.

On 2 July 1460, the Yorkists were welcomed into London by representatives from the clergy, including Cardinal Thomas Bourchier, Archbishop of Canterbury, together with the Bishops of London, Lincoln, Exeter and Salisbury. The Tower of London remained occupied by Lancastrian forces loyal to Henry VI led by Thomas Scales, 7th Baron Scales, Constable of the Tower of London. Warwick and the Yorkist forces had to proceed towards Northampton to confront Henry VI. As the Yorkists were unable to remain in London, a conference at Greyfriars on 3 July and the Guildhall on 4 July was convened between the Yorkist earls and the civil powers that controlled the city. It was agreed that Warwick would leave his father, Salisbury, to besiege the Tower of London, together with Lord Cobham and Sir John Wenlock, supported by forces supplied by the Mayor of London and aldermen.

Scales ordered artillery to be fired into the city, 'cast wild fire into the city, and shot in small guns … and hurt men and women and children in the streets',[30] while the citizens outside responded, 'laid great bombards on the far side of the Thames … and crazed the walls thereof in divers places'.[31] Lord Cobham positioned artillery along the southern bank of the River

---

30. Borman, Tracy, *The Story of the Tower of London* (Merrill, London, 2015), p.79.

31. Ibid., p.79.

The Tower of London. (Author's collection)

Thames, while Wenlock and a mercer named John Harow positioned artillery by St Katherines targeting the eastern walls of the fortress. It was reported that 'much harm was done'.[32]

The Tower of London was completely surrounded and Yorkist patrols on the River Thames ensured that the garrison was completely isolated. One Yorkist knight was captured by Lancastrian troops and taken inside the fortress, where he was 'broken limb by limb'.[33]

Warwick arrived in London with Henry VI on 16 July 1460 as the siege continued. The food supplies within the garrison were severely depleted by 18 July and Scales surrendered the Tower of London to the Yorkists on the condition that he and Robert, 3rd Baron Hungerford, should be given their freedom, while their fellow cohorts be tried. Seven were convicted and beheaded at Tyburn. On 20 July, Sir John Wenlock sent Scales to Westminster for refuge in a barge along the River Thames. On leaving the fortress the barge was apprehended by watermen employed by Warwick and March. Scales was taken across to the southern bank by the Bishop of Winchester's Palace, close to St Mary Overie Dock and just west of the old medieval bridge, where he was murdered and his clothes stolen. Warwick was angry that Scales had been murdered after surrendering himself into his custody. He rode to London to proclaim that no one should steal or murder.

---

32. Gairdner, *Three Fifteenth Century Chronicles*, op. cit., p.74.

33. Ibid., p.74.

26

The Painted Chamber, Westminster Palace

Richard, 3rd Duke of York, presented his claim to the throne of England here in 1460.

During the Wars of the Roses, meetings of the House of Lords would take place in the Painted Chamber, where the sovereign would sit on the throne and listen to debates. It was initially called the King's Chamber, but it was later known as the Painted Chamber because of the decorative wall paintings depicting biblical figures. This spectacular room was destroyed by fire in 1834.

Emboldened by the defeat of the Lancastrians at Northampton, York arrived in Chester from Ireland in mid-September 1460 to assert his right to govern England, not as part of the king's council, but as sovereign. He was now willing to challenge Henry VI and commit treason to claim to be the rightful heir to the throne via the Mortimer lineage.

On 7 October 1460, parliament was summoned in the name of Henry VI in London. A Yorkist-dominated council had been appointed to positions in government and during the following three days all anti-Yorkist Acts of Attainder that were passed in 1459 were revoked. The king sat in the Chair of State in the Painted Chamber, while Warwick's brother, George Neville, Bishop of Exeter, officiated over proceedings in which all the acts passed by parliament when Henry VI transferred his court to Coventry were repealed on the grounds that its members had not been elected.

York arrived in London as if he was king on 10 October. William Worcester recorded that York proceeded 'with 500 horsemen to the Palace of Westminster on the third day of the sitting of Parliament, proclaiming himself by his own mouth heir to the Crown of England'.[34] He entered the Painted Chamber during that day, where he presented his claim to the throne by lineal descent. As he placed his hand on the vacant throne, York anticipated an invitation to sit on it, but the Lords in the Painted Chamber were aghast. York was expecting applause and support, but instead his declaration was received with an uncomfortable silence. The Lords did not expect York to govern the realm and rejected his claim while Henry VI was alive.

---

34. Anonymous, *The Chronicles of the White Rose of York* (James Bohn, London, 1845), p.94.

The Painted Chamber, Palace of Westminster. (William Capon; via Wikimedia Commons)

York had misjudged the political situation and overestimated the level of support from the noblemen. They regarded York as a reformer, a person who could influence change instead of being a potential monarch, nor did they have the appetite to depose Henry VI, who had reigned for thirty-nine years, especially when he was alive and they had already pledged an oath of allegiance. In a combination of pride and arrogance, York had blundered as he created an awkward political situation, totally misreading the judgement of the Lords. He condescendingly left the Painted Chamber, declaring: 'I know no one in this kingdom who would rather come to me.'[35]

After three weeks of debate a compromise was reached when the Act of Accord was passed by Parliament on 25 October 1460, which permitted Henry VI to retain his crown for life, but when he died, the line of succession would not pass to his son, Edward of Westminster, and instead York and his heirs would succeed Henry VI. York would be known as the Prince of Wales and Protector of the Realm. Henry VI, who was imprisoned in London, was forced to agree to the terms of the Act. Gregory affirmed that York 'kept King Harry there [at Westminster] by force and strength, till at the last the king for fear of death granted him the crown, for a man that hath little wit will soon be afraid of death, and yet I trust and believe there was no man that would do him bodily harm'.[36]

The Act of Accord caused further division throughout England and infuriated Queen Margaret, who received the news when she was in Hull. Unlike her weak husband, she refused to acknowledge it. Rejecting the notion that her son would be disinherited and denied his right to the crown, she was determined to oppose the Act and raised an army.

A year after York tried to claim the throne, his eldest son, Edward IV, would open parliament from the Painted Chamber on 4 November 1461, where his title of king was acknowledged, the previous reigns of Henry IV, Henry V and Henry VI were declared illegal and there was a reversal of attainders enacted during the Lancastrian Parliaments.

---

35. Ibid., p.94.

36. Gairdner, *Gregory's Chronicle*, op. cit., p.208.

27

Sandal Castle, Wakefield

Yorkshire Bastion of Richard, 3rd Duke of York, in Wakefield.

Sandal Castle was one of two fortifications built of wood during the twelfth century to defend Wakefield and the bridge across the River Calder. Stone was used during the redevelopment that took place during the thirteenth century and what exists today are those ruins. The castle was fortified with strong walls and surrounded by a deep moat, with the spoils of earth used to construct the mound on which the keep was built. In 1361 Sandal Castle became a royal castle and was a formidable fortress.

Sandal Castle had been owned by the York family since 1347, when Edward III granted it to his son, Edmund of Langley, and it was passed to Richard, 3rd Duke of York. Sandal Castle was in Yorkshire and, although owned by the Yorks, the county was a Lancastrian stronghold.

Five years later, during 1460, Sandal Castle would become a focal point in the Wars of the Roses once again. Margaret raised a force in the Scottish Borders and had publicly remonstrated against the Act of Accord, challenging York to settle the issue of succession through battle. She summoned a council of war among loyal noblemen and announced her intention of marching to London to release Henry VI. On 9 December 1460, York dispatched his eldest son, Edward, Earl of March, to placate Wales and to supress any uprisings led by Jasper Tudor, Earl of Pembroke, who sympathised with the Lancastrians. York proceeded north from London with his son Edmund, Duke of Rutland, and 6,000 men to confront Queen Margaret's forces, leaving Warwick to secure the government in London. York arrived at Sandal Castle on 21 December and received information that Lancastrian forces were holding Pontefract Castle, 9 miles east. Queen Margaret was in Scotland when she sent a force comprising 18,000 men south led by John Clifford, 9th Baron Clifford, and by the time that York had arrived at Sandal Castle, she had reached York. On 28 December, Clifford's forces left Pontefract Castle for Wakefield and York learned that his opponent's forces were more than he had expected. He initially decided to remain inside Sandal Castle until his son, Edward, who was raising a force in the Marches of Wales, could bring reinforcements.

Motte and surviving wall of Sandal Castle. (Author's collection)

The castle was not prepared to receive York and his entourage, so it was necessary for his soldiers to leave the safety of the castle walls to go foraging for food to supplement the meagre supplies during the Christmas season. It demonstrated to the Lancastrians that the Yorkists were in a weakened position. It was from Sandal Castle on 30 December that York led his men from the castle onto the battlefield, which proved to be a fatal mistake. The castle was left unprotected and while the Battle of Wakefield was being fought, James Butler, 1st Earl of Wiltshire, led a detachment to capture it. Eleven years later, Edward IV and Richard, Duke of Gloucester, passed through Sandal Castle on their journey from York to London to confront Warwick at Barnet in 1471.

Sandal Castle continued to play a role during the Wars of the Roses. The Council of the North based itself at Sandal Castle during June 1484. Edward IV had established the council in 1472 as a base to consolidate royal authority in the north of England. Richard, Duke of Gloucester, held the position of first Lord President of the Council of the North from 1472 and during his reign as king until his death in 1485. The council was an additional branch of

Remains of the main gate to Sandal Castle. (Author's collection)

the King's Council, responsible for maintaining law and order in the region. While he was king, Richard ordered that the defences of the castle be strengthened and the accommodation made more comfortable. The castle fell into disrepair during the reign of Elizabeth I and it was ransacked during the English Civil War in 1646.

28

Battlefield at Wakefield

Site of the Lancastrian victory over the Yorkists.

On 30 December 1460, Richard, 3rd Duke of York, moved from the safe confines of Sandal Castle, northwards onto the field that is visible, as shown in the photograph. Much of the battlefield has been built upon, but this was where York was entrapped by Lancastrian forces.

When York arrived at Sandal Castle, it is believed that a truce had been arranged with Henry Beaufort, 3rd Duke of Somerset, and Henry Percy, 3rd Earl of Northumberland, based at Pontefract Castle for the duration of the Christmas period. However, on 30 December 1460, Somerset's forces were facing the northern wall of Sandal Castle. Unbeknown to York, a force led by James Butler, 1st Earl of Wiltshire, were concealed in woods on Somerset's right flank, with cavalry commanded by Thomas Ros, 9th Baron Ros, hidden in woods on the left. York charged downhill from the castle from this site into Somerset's line. It is not known why York would leave a safe, dominant position where he was waiting for reinforcements, instead of placing himself and the Yorkist army in a vulnerable position, where they were ambushed. Possibly, his soldiers ventured beyond the walls of Sandal Castle to search for food when they were attacked while in this vulnerable position, and York and Salisbury rushed forward to rescue them before finding themselves surrounded by the Lancastrians.

York nearly penetrated through Somerset's line and Clifford's reserves had to be brought up from the rear to stop the Yorkist advance. As soon as Wiltshire and Ros advanced behind York from the flanks, York was trapped, the battle lost and Sandal Castle captured.

However, before the battle, during a council of war with his officers, York expressed an intent to leave the safety of Sandal Castle and confront his opponents. According to Edward Hall, his ancestor, a veteran warrior and chief counsellor named Sir David Hall, tried to deter him from this course of action. York responded:

Ah, Davy, Davy, has thou loved me so long, and wouldst now have me dishonoured? No man ever saw me keep a fortress when I was Regent of Normandy, when the Dauphin, with his puissance, came to besiege me; but like a man, and not like a bird enclosed in a

The battlefield at Wakefield where York descended from the defences of Sandal Castle into the field below, where he was ambushed. Somerset was directly ahead of him, with Clifford in the rear. Wiltshire was in a forest to the left of the photo, with cavalry commanded by Ros on the right. (Author's collection)

cage, I issued, and fought with mine enemies; to their loss (I thank God), and ever to my honour. If I have not kept myself within walls for fear of a great and strong prince, nor hid my face from any living mortal, wouldst thou that I should incarcerate and shut myself up for dread of a scolding woman, whose weapons are her tongue and nails. All men would cry wonder and report dishonour, that a woman made a dastard of me, whom no man could ever, to this day, report as a coward. And, surely, my mind is rather to die with honour than live with shame. Their numbers do not appal me. Assuredly, I will fight with them if I fight alone. Therefore, advance my banners in the name of God and St George![37]

By 30 December 1460, York had spent a week inside Sandal Castle and reinforcements did not arrive. He may have preferred to fight instead of starve. There is also the theory that York had been in contact with John Neville, who had raised 8,000 men, and was under the impression that he would join the Yorkist side. On the day of the battle, he may have seen Neville's men approach behind the Lancastrians, and was spurred on by launching a pincer movement. Unbeknown to York, Neville had betrayed him and had joined the Lancastrians.

---

37. Hall, op. cit., p.250.

29

Monument dedicated to Richard, 3rd Duke of York, Wakefield

York was killed at the Battle of Wakefield.

A monument marking the spot where Richard, Duke of York, was killed is situated in Manygates Lane, Wakefield. On it is inscribed 'Richard Plantagenet Duke of York fighting for the cause for the White Rose fell on this spot in the Battle of Wakefield December 30 1460.'

After he left the safety of Sandal Castle, York advanced northwards towards Wakefield, but soon found himself surrounded by his foe and captured, close to where this monument is situated. Today the memorial stands adjacent to Manygates School, which is now an urban area, but in 1460, this was countryside. According to Abbot John Whethamstede, he was brought to an ant hill, where he was made to sit as if it was a throne, before a diadem of knotted grass, representing a crown, was placed upon his head in a mock coronation ceremony. He was scorned and insulted by his captors, who cried 'Hail, King without a kingdom!' before being savagely beheaded.[38]

According to the *Croyland Chronicle*:

> Richard, Duke of York, incautiously engaged the northern army at Wakefield, which was fighting for the king, upon which, a charge was made by the enemy on his men, and he was without mercy or respect relentlessly slain. There fell with him at the same place many noble and illustrious men; and countless numbers of common people, who had followed him, met their deaths there, and all to no purpose.[39]

York died with approximately 2,500 men, while the Lancastrians lost 200 men.[40] Richard Neville, 5th Earl of Salisbury, was captured by soldiers serving Andrew Trollope, taken to Pontefract Castle and executed after the battle.

---

38. Halstead, Caroline A, *Richard III, Volume One* (Longman, London, 1844), p.38.

39. Riley, Henry T., *Ingulph's Chronicle of the Abbey of Croyland* (George Bell & Sons, London, 1908), p.421.

40. Mowat, R.B., *The Wars of the Roses* 1377–1471 (Crosby Lockwood & Son, London, 1914), p.140.

Above left: Richard, Duke of York, Monument, Wakefield. (Author's collection)

Above right: Inscription on the Richard, Duke of York, Monument, Wakefield. (Author's collection)

Although the leader of the Yorkist claim to the throne had been defeated and killed at Wakefield, the cause of the Yorkist dissatisfaction with the way in which England was governed remained. The opposition to the Lancastrian dynasty and its administration had not dissipated. York's determined, strong-willed, eldest surviving son, Edward, supported by the formidable, capable Richard Neville, 16th Earl of Warwick, was in a position to pick up the baton to galvanise Yorkist sentiment in English towns and continue to challenge Henry VI and his corrupt advisors. Despite claiming his right to the crown of England, York never achieved his aim, however his descendants would succeed where he failed, for he was the father of two kings, Edward IV and Richard III, and the grandfather of Edward V.

After his victory in Towton in 1461, Edward IV ordered that a wooden cross be erected at Wakefield to commemorate his father's last stand. This marker was lost during a siege by Parliament forces of the Royalist-occupied Sandal Castle in 1645 during the English Civil War. The monument that now stands in Manygates Lane was erected in 1897.

30

Old Wakefield Bridge

Edmund, Earl of Rutland, captured and killed.

The Chapel of St Mary the Virgin adjacent to old Wakefield Bridge was constructed in 1397. Edmund, Earl of Rutland, was killed by John Clifford, 9th Baron Clifford, after the Battle of Wakefield on 30 December 1460.

After York was defeated at Wakefield, his son Edmund, Earl of Rutland, aged 17, tried to escape with Sir Thomas Neville, son of the 5th Earl of Salisbury, by fleeing in the direction of Wakefield. Accompanied by Sir Robert Aspall, Edmund's tutor and chaplain to his father, they reached old Wakefield Bridge, which crossed the River Calder, where they were captured by Lancastrian forces commanded by Clifford. It is believed

Chapel of St Mary the Virgin and the Old Wakefield Bridge. (Author's collection)

'The Murder of Rutland' by Charles Robert Leslie, 1815. (Pennsylvania Academy of the Fine Arts/Public Domain)

that they were trying to get to the chapel on the north part of the bridge to seek sanctuary. According to Edward Hall, Edmund pleaded for his life to be spared with Clifford, to no avail. Clifford was seeking vengeance and retorted: 'By God's blood, thy father slew mine, and so will I do thee and all thy kin,'[41] before brutally killing him with a dagger into his heart. Clifford, who would earn a reputation as 'the Butcher', told the priest to inform his mother and brother of Edmund's death. Clifford had avenged the House of York for their part in the death of his father, Thomas, 8th Baron Clifford, at the First Battle of St Albans in 1455. The executions of prominent Yorkist figures at Wakefield plunged this feud between the House of York and Lancaster to a sinister depth, and brought the conflict to a position where optimism for reconciliation was lost.

---

41. Hall, op. cit., p.251.

31

Micklegate Bar, York

The heads of Yorkist leaders impaled upon the battlements of Micklegate Bar.

Micklegate Bar was built during the early twelfth century, but a gateway had existed on the site since the Roman occupation. The height of the gatehouse was increased in 1350 with a barbican and portcullis, together with an outer passage way. Monarchs were greeted on entry to York at Micklegate Bar and it was the place where the heads of traitors were displayed upon the battlements.

Micklegate Bar has strong associations with the Wars of the Roses. After being killed on the battlefield at Wakefield, the body of Richard, 3rd Duke of York, was brought to York on 31 December 1460, the day after the battle. His decapitated head was placed on a lance and presented to Queen Margaret. She ordered that a paper crown be placed upon his head and it was placed upon a spike on the battlements of Micklegate Bar. The paper crown was meant to ridicule his claim for her husband's throne. Margaret also ordered that a sign be placed below his severed head with the words 'Let York overlook York'. The bodies of York's son, Edmund, Earl of Rutland, the 5th Earl of Salisbury, and his son, Sir Thomas Neville, also suffered the same fate, being beheaded and their heads displayed alongside the head of York, where they were to remain for three months.

This occurred when Richard (the future King Richard III) was seven years old and must have had a devastating impact upon him to hear of the deaths of his father (Richard, Duke of York), brother (Rutland) and uncle (Salisbury), as well as the disrespect shown to their corpses. For Richard's elder brother, Edward, this outrageous act would incite him to avenge their deaths and escalate the conflict, for he would enter York via Micklegate Bar victorious on 30 March 1461, the day after defeating the Lancastrians at Towton. He ordered that the heads of his father and brother be removed from Micklegate Bar and their bodies interred in Pontefract Castle. Their heads were replaced with the heads of the Lancastrian noblemen including, Thomas Courtenay, 14th Earl of Devon, who was captured at Towton and executed in York on 3 April 1461.

On 29 August 1483, Richard III entered through Micklegate Bar as King of England with his queen, Anne Neville, and son, Prince Edward of Middleham, during his Royal progress.

He was greeted by civic dignitaries, who were ordered to wear ceremonial scarlet, while the citizens of York were instructed to hang colourful fabrics from their shops and homes along the procession route from Micklegate Bar to York Minster.

Today Micklegate Bar houses the Henry VII Experience, which is a permanent museum devoted to the first Tudor monarch. It is administered by the York Archaeological Trust in conjunction with the Richard III Experience, which can be visited at Monks Bar, York.

Micklegate Bar, York. (Serg Zastavkin/Shutterstock)

32

Battle of Mortimer's Cross Monument

First battle fought by Edward, Earl of March.

Edward, Earl of March, was in Gloucester, preparing to resist a potential Lancastrian uprising led by Jasper Tudor, Earl of Pembroke, stepbrother of Henry VI, when he received the news that his brother, Edmund, and father, Richard, had been killed at Wakefield.

March was aged 18 when he succeeded his father as 4th Duke of York and he received messages of encouragement to challenge Henry VI. Support for Henry VI was diminishing, according to the *Croyland Chronicle*, after him reigning for thirty-nine years:

> their hearts were no longer with him, nor, would they any longer admit of his being king. Besides, in consequence of a malady that had been for many years increasing upon him, he had fallen into a weak state of mind, and had for a length of time remained in a state of imbecility and held the government in name only. Upon this, the nobles and people immediately sent special messengers into Wales to the before named Earl of March, in whom they could place entire confidence, to disclose to him the wishes of the people, and request him, with earnest entreaties, to hasten into England to their speedy succour, as further delay only seemed to increase their perils.[42]

Buoyed by the support of the people, during January 1461 March raised an army amounting to 23,000 men,[43] according to some chroniclers, to avenge their deaths and continue the Yorkist claim to the throne. The *Croyland Chronicle* recorded that March 'was now in the flower of his age, tall of stature, elegant in person, of unblemished character, valiant in arms, and a lineal descendant of the illustrious line of King Edward the Third'.[44] March led his army to the Midlands to join forces with Richard Neville, 16th Earl of Warwick, and descend upon

---

42. Riley, *Croyland*, op. cit., p.424.
43. Brooke, Richard, *Visits to Fields of Battle in England of the Fifteenth Century* (J.R. Smith, London, 1857), p.73.
44. Riley, *Croyland*, op. cit., p.424.

Battle of Mortimer Cross Monument, Kingsland, Herefordshire. (Courtesy of Jeff Tomlinson; www.geograph.org.uk)

London before the Lancastrians arrived. On reaching Hereford, March received news that Pembroke, together with James Butler, 1st Earl of Wiltshire, had mustered a strong force comprising Irish, Bretons and Frenchmen in Wales. Although they were followed by this small Lancastrian army, March feared being surrounded if attacked by another enemy force, so he decided to turn back to confront them. On 2 February 1461, March engaged with Pembroke's forces at Mortimer's Cross, which is situated between Ludlow and Hereford. According to Hall, during the morning prior to the battle, three suns appeared and converged into one, at which point Edward, on his knees, prayed and thanked God.[45] March viewed this omen as divine endorsement and spurred his courage. Edward may have seen the meteorological phenomenon known as a 'sun dog' or 'parhelion', which is an illusion of multiple suns.

---

45. Hall, op. cit., p.251.

Edward IV Sun Emblem Badge. It is conjectured that the vision of the three suns seen by Edward, Earl of March, on the morning before the Battle of Mortimer's Cross inspired him to adopt the sun emblem for his own motif. When he became king, his supporters wore this sun emblem badge to show their allegiance. Shakespeare alluded to this in the opening soliloquy in Richard III when he referred to the 'sun of York'. However, the shining sun had been used as a royal emblem since the reign of Richard II. (Author's collection)

March's forces killed approximately 3,800 Lancastrians.[46] Some of the captains who were captured were executed after the battle. Pembroke and Wiltshire fled the battlefield in disguise. This was March's first experience in battle and as a commander. It was also the first step towards claiming the throne for the Yorkists. After his victory at Mortimer's Cross, March continued to march upon London to join Warwick.

This monument was erected in 1799 to commemorate the Battle of Mortimer's Cross in Kingsland, Herefordshire.

---

46. Brooke, op. cit., p.73.

33

Marketplace at St Albans

Lancastrian victory on 17 February 1461.

This view is from the clocktower looking north-east towards St Peter's Church, where Warwick deployed his Yorkist forces astride St Peter's Street by this church during the second Battle of St Albans. Warwick's archers were also positioned around the clocktower in the marketplace, where they resisted an attempt made by Lancastrian soldiers led by Captain Andrew Trollope to attack Warwick from the rear.

As Edward, Earl of March, headed for London after his victory at Mortimer's Cross, Henry Beaufort, 3rd Duke of Somerset, was leading the Lancastrian army with Queen Margaret from York towards the capital in an initiative to rescue Henry VI from captivity. During February 1461, Warwick led a contingent of the Yorkist army northwards from London to prevent the Lancastrians reaching London. The opposing armies both comprised of 5,000 soldiers. Warwick sent part of his army to Dunstable, while he held positions at St Albans. Warwick brought the captive Henry VI with him to St Albans. Queen Margaret received intelligence of Warwick's position, which was close to St Peter's Church. She surrounded Yorkist forces in Dunstable on 16 February 1461 before confronting Warwick at St Albans on the following day. Captain Anthony Trollope, the veteran soldier, was at the head of the Lancastrian vanguard.

Warwick stationed some of his army outside St Albans at Bernards Heath, while he held a line with his archers in St Peter's Street in the town. Trollope led a detachment that skirted the north of the town to St Michael's Church, near Verulamium Park, then turned south-east, uphill into the town, where it attacked Warwick's position from the rear. Although taken by surprise, the archers managed to resist the first wave of the Lancastrian assault at the Market Cross, close to the clocktower. Musketeers from Flanders were serving alongside the Yorkist army. Using a musket on a stand, their weapons caused them more harm than upon their foe, because as they fired at the Lancastrians, the wind was blowing in their direction, causing the flame discharged from their muskets to blow in their faces and burning some of them to death.

Trollope's men retreated back down the hill before heading east and then re-entered the town via Folly Lane and Catherine Street, and then onto St Peter's Street. From there they attacked the main body of Warwick's men and secured St Albans. The Yorkists became overwhelmed

The view from the clocktower looking north-east towards St Peter's Church, where it is believed soldiers killed during the First Battle of St Albans were buried. Soldiers of York and Lancaster fought on the streets that you see below during both battles. Although the shops and houses are modern, the streets and alleyways have remained as they were during the 15th century. The two lanes join each other to the marketplace, where the white building now houses the St Albans Museum. This was where Henry VI was wounded during the first battle in 1455. During the second battle in 1461, Warwick deployed his forces astride St Peter's Street close to St Peter's Church. The church tower can be seen in the photo. (Author's collection)

and their line was struggling to hold its position. Sir Henry Lovelace, Captain of the Kent detachment and his followers, defected to the Lancastrian side, which caused much disruption. It was here that Warwick's left flank collapsed and he was forced to flee westwards towards Oxfordshire with the intention of joining forces with March.

Henry VI was abandoned by the Yorkists and found under a tree talking to himself, while other accounts reported that he crossed the lines to his own side. After the battle he was reunited with his family. He knighted his son Edward, Prince of Wales, and Andrew Trollope, the veteran Lancastrian soldier. Trollope was wounded in the foot by a caltrop, which was a device made of iron with spikes, devised to wound the feet of horses. Trollope responded to receiving the honour with the words 'My Lord, I have not deserved it for I slew but 15 men, for I stood still in one place and they come unto me, but they bode still with me.'[47]

---

47. Gairdner, *Gregory's Chronicle*, op. cit., p.214.

The fate of the captured Sir Thomas Kyriell, together with his son, was decided by Edward, Prince of Wales, when his mother asked, 'Fair son, with what death shall these two knights die whom you see there?' and the prince decreed 'that their heads should be cut off'.[48] Margaret showed no mercy for her rivals and this cruelty and callousness in getting her son, aged 8, to make the decision, was, although perceived as inhuman today, Margaret's method of educating Edward and teaching him a lesson in survival and the need to be strong as king. The executions were conducted before the queen and her son.

Among those killed on the Lancastrian side at St Albans was Sir John Grey. He had been knighted during the day before the battle and was the husband of Elizabeth Woodville, who would marry his adversary, Edward IV, during May 1464. Lord Bonneville and Sir Thomas Kyriell, who were executed, were the king's bodyguards. John Neville was spared because he had served as the king's chamberlain. Other accounts suggest that the Yorkists lost 200 men. Somerset, the victor of the Second Battle of St Albans, avenged the death of his father, who had been killed during the first battle for the town six years earlier.

Abbot Whethamstede appealed to Henry VI in St Albans Abbey to issue a decree against plundering the town, for which he did, but because the king was so timid and lacked authority, his own soldiers ignored his order and proceeded to pillage St Albans. Queen Margaret remained in St Albans for nine days while negotiations for the surrender of London were taking place. London was 20 miles south from the town and the populace feared that the Lancastrians would plunder the city and refused to open its gates. Instead of advancing upon the capital, Henry VI and Margaret headed north towards York, where her army plundered its way along the journey.

---

48. Mowat, op. cit., p.148.

34

Crossing at Ferrybridge

Prelude to Towton.

The stone bridge, built during 1804, marks the site of a wooden bridge that was the focal point for the Battle of Ferrybridge.

Edward, Earl of March, took possession of the crown and sceptre at Westminster Abbey on 4 March 1461 and was now Edward IV. Before being crowned he wanted to defeat Margaret once and for all, otherwise his position as king would not be secure. He sent his uncle, William Neville, 6th Baron Fauconberg; John Mowbray, 3rd Duke of Norfolk; and Richard Neville, 16th Earl of Warwick; to assemble troops and march north in order to confront Margaret. Edward followed them, departing from London on 12 March 1461.

On 28 March 1461, Yorkist forces commanded by Warwick and with his second in command, John Radcliffe, Lord Fitzwalter, leading the vanguard, reached the River Aire at Ferrybridge where the Great North Road crossed the River Aire. The wooden bridge was held by soldiers belonging to the 9th Baron Clifford on the northern bank. The river was wide and deep and the only way that it could be crossed was to launch a direct assault upon the bridge. The Lancastrians had sabotaged the structure, rendering it unstable, and as Yorkist soldiers tried to cross the river, it came under fire from Lancastrian archers. Many Yorkists fell into the freezing water of the Aire and drowned. Fitzwalter was among those killed, while Warwick sustained an arrow wound to his leg. Edward IV had reached Pontefract Castle on that day and he sent soldiers to aid Warwick. Another attempt to secure the bridge was launched at midday and six hours of hard fighting ensued before it fell into the hands of the Yorkists. Baron Fauconberg had crossed the river 3 miles upstream at Castleford and attacked the Lancastrians from the rear. George Neville wrote to Francisco Coppini, Bishop of Terni, Apostolic Legate in Flanders:

> At Ferrybridge … the attack commenced. The enemy had broken the ferry-bridge and, occupying the narrow raft which our people had made after its destruction by handicraft, they stoutly disputed its passage but we carried it sword in hand.[49]

---

49. Brown, Rawdon Lubbock, *Calendar of state papers and manuscripts, relating to English affairs existing in the archives and collection of Venice, and in other libraries of northern Italy, Volume 1, 1202-1509* (Longman, London, 1864), p.99.

View from the southern bank of the River Aire, where Yorkist solders crossed the damaged wooden bridge. (Author's collection)

Despite the Lancastrians defending the eastern bank of the Aire, the Yorkists broke through with many slain on both sides. According to Wavrin, 'the battle lasted from midday to six o'clock in the evening and there died more than 3,000 men on both sides'.[50]

The Yorkist army passed over the bridge and Fauconberg pursued the fleeing Lancastrians towards Towton. Clifford fled Ferrybridge and was pursued to Saxton, south of Towton, where he had removed his gorget, which restricted his ability to fight. This left his throat exposed and he was killed by an arrow.

The deaths of John, 9th Baron Clifford, his brother's murderer at Wakefield, and John, Baron Neville, whose defection to the Lancastrians at Wakefield betrayed his father, must have buoyed the spirits and confidence of Edward IV and his followers as they approached Towton.

---

50. Wavrin, John de, *A Collection of Chronicle and Ancient Histories of Great Britain, now called England* Vol. 3 (London, 1864–87), p.337.

35

St Mary's Church, Lead

Edward IV's Yorkist army camped here before and after the Battle of Towton.

During the morning of Palm Sunday, 29 March 1461, the Yorkist army arrived at Lead, just south of Towton. The church and surrounding fields around St Mary's Church at Lead was an assembly position for the Yorkist armies where they waited in the snow to engage in battle.

Some of the men who had marched from London had fought the previous day to secure the crossing across the Aire at Ferrybridge and would have been exhausted, hungry and anxious as they looked towards the ridge north-east of their position. The Lancastrian army held the advantage of the high ground and the Yorkists had a difficult task ahead as they would need to ascend this ridge in the snow in order to assault the position. Conscious that it was Palm Sunday, Henry VI offered a truce, but Edward declined his offer.

According to Richard Brooke, John, Baron Neville, was buried at this chapel in Lead after he was killed during the pursuit from Ferrybridge but there is no monument dedicated to his memory.[51]

---

51. Brooke, Richard, *Visits to Fields of Battle in England of the Fifteenth Century* (J.R. Smith, London, 1857), p.125.

St Mary's Church, Lead. (Author's collection)

36

Towton Memorial Cross

The largest battle fought on English soil.

The plinth that is situated adjacent to the B1217 is modern, but the cross is medieval. The base of the monument is becoming illegible due to erosion, but reads 'Battle of Towton, Palm Sunday, 1461'. Known locally as Lord Dacre's Cross, the Towton Memorial stands behind the rear of the Lancastrian line during the Battle of Towton. The memorial marks one of the bloodiest battles ever fought in England where an estimated 50,000 soldiers fought for ten hours, of which 28,000 perished.

The Battle of Towton began at 9.00 am on 29 March 1461. Edward IV was significantly outnumbered by the Lancastrian forces. Fauconberg led the Yorkist vanguard with a detachment of archers, followed by Warwick. Forces commanded by Sir John Wenlock, on the left flank, with Sir John Dynham on the right flank advancing behind Warwick, while Edward IV brought up the rear. Edward had issued the proclamation before the battle that no prisoners were to be taken. A similar edict was adopted by the Lancastrian side. Looking northwards from Saxton, Sir Andrew Trollope carried the left flank opposing Wenlock, while Henry Percy, 3rd Earl of Northumberland, held the right flank opposite Dynham. Sections commanded by Somerset and Henry Holland 3rd Duke of Exeter, followed behind them. The Towton Memorial Cross is positioned where the rear lines of the Lancastrian soldiers stood on the day of the battle.

Fauconberg's column advanced and as they got to within range of the vanguard of the Lancastrian lines, he ordered his archers to shoot one flight of arrows and then stop. The Lancastrians misjudged their position and shot their arrows inaccurately in the direction of Fauconberg's line. Although the Yorkists were disadvantaged as they ascended the high ground, the sleet and wind were blowing in the faces of Lancastrian archers, and the wind meant their arrows fell short of their opposing foe. As soon as the Lancastrian arrows fell to the ground, Fauconberg ordered his archers to retrieve them. The Lancastrian archers soon expended their supplies of arrows and they were in a vulnerable situation. Fauconberg ordered his archers to advance and not only shoot their own arrows, but those that they had gathered from the ground, which they did with deadly effect. Once Fauconberg's archers had used all their arrows, Edward ordered the entire Yorkist army onto the battlefield armed with maces, mallets, axes

Towton Memorial Cross, North Yorkshire, marking the site where the Houses of York and Lancaster battled in the snow for the English crown on Palm Sunday, 1461. (Author's collection)

and swords, and a bitter battle ensued for ten hours. The *Croyland Chronicle* referred to the Battle of Towton where 'engaged in most severe conflict and fighting hand to hand with sword and spear, there was no small slaughter on either side'.[52]

The battle was so brutal and the carnage so immense that the opposing sides had to temporarily stop fighting in order to clear the bodies before they continued. Edward IV, dressed in armour, was in command of the reserve column and went along the line entering the battle to bolster weaknesses, comforting his men and caring for the wounded. He fought in the thick of the battle, as George Neville wrote: 'I prefer you should learn from others than myself how manfully, our King, the Duke of Norfolk, and nay my brother and uncle bore themselves in this battle; first fighting like common soldiers, then commanding, encouraging, and rallying their squadrons like the greatest captains.'[53]

Richard Beauchamp, Bishop of Salisbury, also commented upon the bravery of Edward IV that 'so great was the power and impetus of the enemy, had not the prince single-handed put himself forward so notably as he did, with the utmost of human courage'.[54]

---

52. Riley, *Croyland*, op. cit., p.425.

53. Brown, op. cit., p.100.

54. Ibid., p.101.

37

Bloody Meadow, Towton

Site of the Lancastrian massacre.

As the Yorkist army broke through, the Lancastrians were pushed off the ridge into Bloody Meadow. It was here that the white snow was saturated with the red blood of Lancastrian soldiers who were fleeing for their lives from their pursuing foe.

The Lancastrians attacked from the west from Castle Hill Wood around midday on 30 March 1461, outflanking the Yorkists with superior numbers. As the afternoon progressed the Yorkist left flank was close to collapsing as it was pushed towards eastwards to where the Towton Memorial now stands. The Yorkists held on until 4.00 pm, when 5,000 reinforcements belonging to John Mowbray, 3rd Duke of Norfolk, arrived at the right time to strengthen the Yorkist position and overwhelm the weary Lancastrians. This was a pivotal moment in the battle as within an hour the line buckled and the Yorkists pushed the Lancastrians across the Saxton–Towton Road, forcing a disorderly retreat, west from the Towton Memorial, towards Bloody Meadow and the steep banks of the River Cock. The path of the retreating Lancastrians can be followed by walking west along the track from the Towton Memorial, where the Towton Battlefield Society has installed information boards. It was from here that the steep decline into Bloody Meadow can be seen. The descent would have been complicated by snow and ice on the day of the battle and many of those in flight would have stumbled and slipped down this bank. Those who maintained their balance would have been fleeing from pursuing Yorkist soldiers, hell bent on killing their foe irrespective of whether they were common soldiers or commanders. Those that fell were slaughtered on the ground. Those that were still on their feet ran west, where they encountered the swollen river, the Cock Beck, and many drowned. The *Croyland Chronicle* depicts an image of how the Towton battlefield looked on Palm Sunday in 1461, and why this hallowed ground is known as Bloody Meadow:

> The blood, too, of the slain, mingling with the snow which at this time covered the whole surface of the earth, afterwards ran down in the furrows and ditches along the melted snow, in a most shocking manner, for a distance of two or three miles.[55]

---

55. Riley, *Croyland*, op. cit., p.426.

Bloody Meadow and Castle Hill Wood. This photograph was taken from the Bloody Meadow information board looking south-west, towards Castle Hill Wood, which is the wood in the centre in the distance and is significantly reduced since the battle. This was where the Lancastrians led a counter-attack against the rear of the Yorkist line, from right to left, during the Battle of Towton. The trees in the valley in the foreground line the river known as the Cock Beck, which flows through Bloody Meadow and was the site where the Lancastrians were routed by the Yorkists. (Author's collection)

George Neville claimed that 'very many were killed on both sides, but at length the enemy showed their backs and many fell in the flight. That day's battle was a great one for it commenced about sunrise and lasted till about ten o'clock at night, such was the obstinacy and boldness of mortal men on the verge of a wretched death.'[56]

---

56. Brown, op. cit., pp.99–100.

38

Wooden bridge over the Cock Beck, Towton

Site of carnage on Palm Sunday, 1461.

The Cock Beck is a stream that flows through Bloody Meadow and although narrow, it was deep and a formidable natural obstacle, covered in snow, for the fleeing Lancastrians to cross as they were being pursued and cut down by their Yorkist foe.

As soon as the Lancastrian line had broken, Edward directed his cavalry to pursue them, revising his order that no prisoners to be taken, ordering that no enemy commanders be taken and that the common soldiers were to be spared. This order was disregarded as the Lancastrians who were holding the left flank retreated in a north-westerly direction towards Towton and Tadcaster, while those on the right flank were chased down into Bloody Meadow and the Cock Beck.

Once the Lancastrian line had been broken, its soldiers were forced to flee the battlefield or be slain. The *Croyland Chronicle* commented: 'their ranks being now broken and scattered in flight, the king's army eagerly pursued them, cutting down the fugitives with their swords, just like so many sheep for the slaughter'.[57]

The Lancastrian corpses were so many that they were piled up in the stream, acting as a ford and enabling the survivors to cross and flee the battlefield over this gruesome bridge. The water of the Cock Beck was red with blood. The number of deaths at Towton was unprecedented on English soil. Richard Beauchamp, Bishop of Salisbury, wrote, 'there consequently perished a number of men, nearly … hitherto unheard of in our country, and estimated by the heralds at 28,000, besides the wounded and those who were drowned'.[58]

Sir Andrew Trollope and Henry Percy, 3rd Earl of Northumberland, were among the Lancastrian commanders who fell during the battle. Despite the order to take no prisoners, forty-two Lancastrian knights were captured, but were later executed to prevent future rebellions.

---

57. Riley, *Croyland*, op. cit., p.425.

58. Brown, op. cit., p.102.

Wooden bridge over the Cock Beck where fleeing Lancastrians were slaughtered or drowned. The massacre was immense and the Cock Beck flowed red with blood. (Courtesy of Ian S; www.geograph.org.uk)

The Battle of Towton would bring peace to England for the next nine years. Edward had fought for the crown and the path was now clear for his coronation at Westminster Abbey. Richard Beauchamp exclaimed that 'the entire realm now acknowledges one sovereign and the power of others has utterly vanished'.[59]

Henry VI, Margaret and Prince Edward were in York and when Exeter and Somerset arrived with news of the Lancastrian defeat at Towton, they fled for their lives to Scotland. In exchange for sanctuary, Henry VI surrendered the garrison of Berwick. Edward IV arrived in York shortly after the battle, where he released John Neville, Warwick's brother, who was captured at the Second Battle of St Albans. Edward rested in York for three weeks before heading north to Newcastle, where during May he ordered the beheading of James Butler, 1st Earl of Wiltshire. He had abandoned his men on the battlefield on three occasions – at the First Battle of St Albans, at Mortimer's Cross and Towton – but fate had caught the cowardly Earl. His head was set upon London Bridge as a traitor. Edward then turned south to return to London for his coronation at Westminster Abbey.

---

59. Brown, op. cit., p.101.

39

The Towton Skeleton

A casualty of Towton.

The remains of this soldier were discovered beneath Towton Hall, which was north of the battlefield. He was one of 50,000 soldiers that fought at Towton. This was the path used by retreating Lancastrian soldiers who were carrying the left flank during the battle and any of the fallen were buried in mass graves within the vicinity of where Towton Hall is situated. This area was later called Chapel Hill because during 1483 Richard III ordered that a chapel be constructed here to commemorate those soldiers buried here and his brother, Edward IV's victory, but the building was not completed after his death at Bosworth.

During the building of an extension on the north-east side of Towton Hall in July 1996 a burial pit containing twenty-three bodies was uncovered and they were exhumed and reinterred in Saxton churchyard. Several mass graves were found within the vicinity during further construction work in that same month. North Yorkshire County Council Heritage Unit was summoned to inspect the site and the developer gave permission for an archaeological excavation to be carried out on one of the graves. The remains of forty-three bodies were uncovered and lay in the pit in a south-east to north-west direction, with the heads facing west. They were found in a shallow rectangular pit; their clothes were stripped and they had been thrown into it without respect or ceremony. The bodies were recovered and transferred to the University of Bradford for further analysis.

Archaeologists were able to discover information about the fate of these soldiers who were killed at Towton. This skeleton of an unknown soldier was found beneath Towton Hall with two other bodies. It is exhibited at the Richard III Experience at Monk's Bar, York, and was among those investigated. It is difficult to determine on which side this soldier fought, but given that he was found a mile north of the battlefield, it is certain that he was killed as the Lancastrians withdrew and it is probable that he was a Lancastrian. He was aged between 36 and 45 when he died and was 6ft 1in tall. It was probable that he was of high status, but the evidence of the injuries sustained showed that he died a horrific death. He had received a stab wound to the left foot, which splintered one bone, and he received cuts to two other bones that suggest could have been on horseback and his foe was attacking him from below. Three wounds on his skull were also found, including his lower jaw, which was slashed by a blunt weapon and by a sharp instrument. It is hypothesised that a blow to the back of his skull killed him. He may have been unhorsed at the moment of death. He also sustained a blade injury to his right hand. The Towton skeletons also uncovered pathological information about medieval soldiers. This man's remains showed inflammation of the shins, which could be attributed to long marches, and Schmorl's nodes were found in the spine, which were caused by carrying heavy loads on the back.

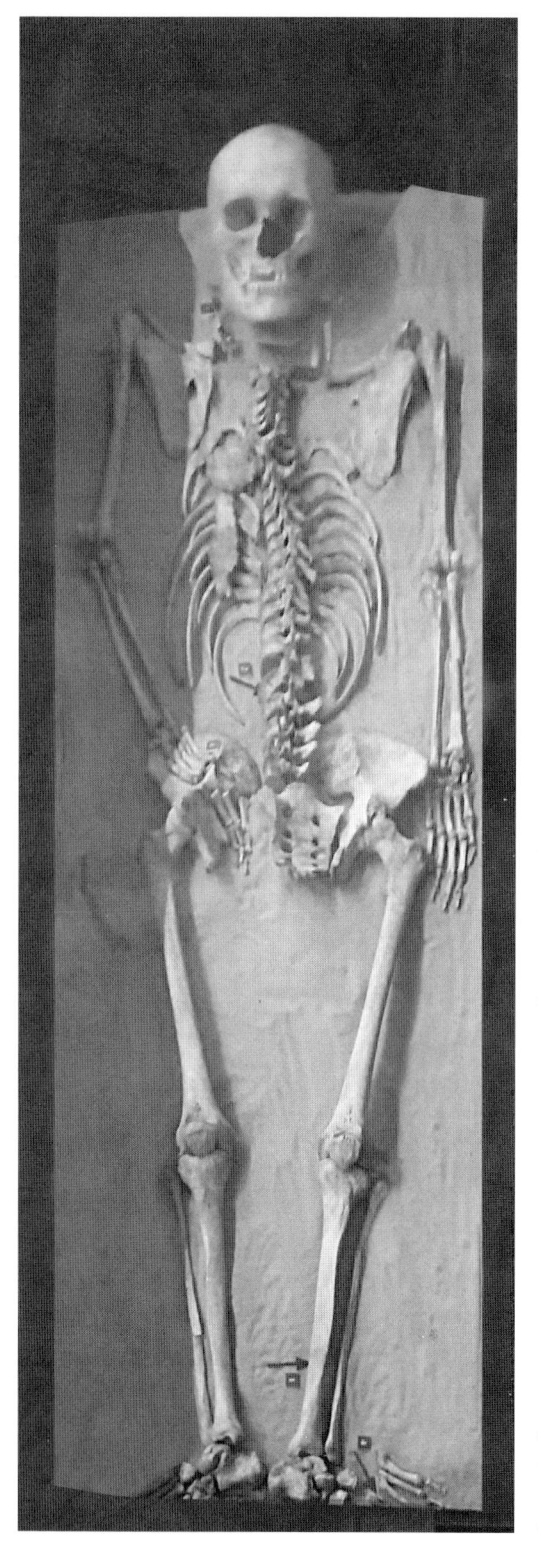

Many of the skulls had multiple injuries caused by sharp weapons such as swords and daggers, as well as blunt instruments such as maces and hammers. It was thought that the victims were subjected to repeated blows. Some of the injuries were inflicted upon the arms and hands, which indicate that these soldiers were shielding their heads before being struck by the fatal blow. It was possible that these men were captured, their protective headgear removed and then executed after the battle. This theory could be disputed due to the fact that these skeletons do not show any wounds on the lower torso, which suggests that they were wearing armour, and if they were captured and massacred, this protection would have been removed. So it is probable that they were killed fighting for their lives as they retreated.

A skeleton of a soldier killed at the Battle of Towton, displayed at the Richard III Experience, Monks Bar, York. (Author's collection)

40

All Saints Church, Saxton & Lord Dacre's Tomb

Burial site of the fallen from the Battle of Towton.

The Lancastrian army suffered heavy casualties among the men and the noblemen that commanded them. Lord Dacre was among those killed and he was buried in All Saints Saxton Church, south of the Towton battlefield, where his tomb can be visited 500 years later. The tomb is a rare example of a dignified burial at Towton as many of his comrades in arms were buried in large pits on and around the battlefield.

Local tradition has passed down the story that Lord Dacre retired momentarily from the battlefield for respite and refreshment. As he removed his helmet to drink, he was killed by a boy perched in a bur tree armed with a crossbow, the arrow thrusting into his neck. Folklore has intimated that the bur tree that stands solitary on the battleground today was a descendent of this vantage point.

Dacre was buried with his horse and during 1861 the head of a horse was found close to his tomb. There is a legend that states that Dacre was buried upright astride his horse, while Brooke mentions that he was buried standing in an upright position.

Dacre was among many noblemen who were killed at Towton. Nicholas O'Flanagan, Bishop of Elphin, noted down the casualties at Towton in a letter to the Bishop of Teramo, Papal Legate:

> King Edward IV gained a victory over his enemies on Palm Sunday. The list of those who were killed is overleaf, namely the Earls of Northumberland and Devon, the Lords de Clifford, de Beaumont, Dacre, de Willoughby, de Welles and de Scales, Anthony de Ryvers [Rivers], Lord Maley (Mauley), Rafe Bygot, Lord Nevill, Lord Henry, son of the Duke of Buckingham, Sir Rafe Percy, Sir Thomas Bellingham, Sir Andrew Trolopp [Trollope], Sir William Bastard of Exeter. The number of commoners killed on the other side was 28,000, while on King Edward's side only one lord was killed, Lord Fitzwalter, and 800 men of the commons.[60]

---

60. Brown, op. cit., p.103.

Left: Lord Dacre's Tomb at Saxton Church. (Author's collection)

Below: All Saints Church, Saxton. (Author's collection)

After the battle, the gruesome task of recovering and burying the dead took place. The *Croyland Chronicle* confirmed that many of the fallen were 'piled up in pits and in trenches prepared for the purpose'.[61] One such pit was dug within Saxton churchyard. A burial mound was found north of the church in 1804 and is believed to contain the graves of knights killed during the battle. Fifty years later, Richard Brooke wrote after visiting the church:

> Great numbers of the slain were interred in Saxton Churchyard, in a large trench or pit on the north side of the church. Their bones were exposed to view, lying about four feet below the surface, in making a vault not many years ago, and again, subsequently, in making another, in 1848; we may conclude that they were the bones of the Yorkists of some consideration, from the circumstance of the survivors taking the trouble of interring the remains in consecrated ground, at some little difference from the field of the battle. The persons whose bones were so exposed, must have been either young, or in the prime of life, because the skulls were remarkable for the soundness and excellence of the teeth.[62]

The remains of the Towton soldiers found at Towton Hall were interred close to Lord Dacre's tomb in a mass grave, which is commemorated with a memorial stone. The following words are inscribed on that stone: 'Here lie the remains of unknown soldiers found at Towton Hall 1996 – and killed at the Battle of Towton Palm Sunday 29th March 1461. Remember and pray for all those who died.'

The Yorkists also lost high-profile commanders. A letter received by Pigello Portinari confirmed that Edward IV lost two Lords, John le Scrope and Lord John Fitzwalter, and 8,000 men on the Yorkist side.[63]

---

61. Riley, *Croyland*, op. cit., p.425.
62. Brooke, op. cit., p.98.
63. Brown, op. cit., p.105.

41

Chapel of St John the Evangelist, Tower of London

In this chapel, Edward IV invested his brothers, George and Richard (the future Richard III), as Knights of the Bath.

Built during 1077–97, St John's Chapel is on the second floor of the White Tower. It was one of the earliest Norman churches and was used by the Royal family when they held court or resided at the Tower of London. On 4 November 1429, Henry VI, aged 8, anointed thirty-two knights to the Order of the Bath prior to his coronation. Thirty-two years later Edward IV returned to the Tower of London to perform the same ceremony at St John's Chapel.

The Yorkist victory at Towton meant that it was safe for exiled members of the House of York to return home. Edward IV summoned his mother, Cecily, and his younger brothers, Richard and George, to return to London from exile in Utrecht to attend the coronation ceremony. The family was reunited at the palace at Sheen, now known as Richmond, and it was from here that Edward IV, accompanied by Richard and George, rode triumphantly to the Tower of London on 26 June 1461, where during the evening he entertained with opulence nobles who had supported the House of York. It was also in the Tower of London, in St John's Chapel, two days before the coronation, that Edward invested his younger brothers alongside thirty other nobles as Knights of the Bath.[64]

Richard was aged 8 and too young to appreciate the chivalric tradition that Edward IV wanted to maintain. Two governors escorted Richard into a chamber, where he entered a bath that had been prepared for him. Three Knights of the Order of Bath entered the chamber and the leading knight sprinkled some water over his shoulders and explained the rites and values of the Order. After exiting the bath, he was dried and clothed, assisted by a barber, who was rewarded by being allowed to use the bath that Richard had vacated. Richard was then taken into St John's Chapel, where in the presence of a priest, Richard held a knightly vigil that

---

64. Bayley, John, *The History & Antiquities of the Tower of London* (Jennings and Chaplin, London, 1830), p.44.

Chapel of St John the Evangelist, Tower of London. (Author's collection)

concluded at sunrise with confession and a mass. He was allowed to retire to bed for a brief period to sleep before the final part of the ceremony. This involved Richard riding behind a boy carrying his spurs and sword across the courtyard to the Royal apartments of the Tower of London, where he was presented to Edward IV. At the king's command, two knights attached the spurs to Richard's heels. Edward knighted Richard with a sword, kissed him and said 'Be thou a good knight'. Richard returned to St John's Chapel, where at the high altar he did swear to uphold the rights of the Church. He then attended dinner, but was not permitted to eat. This was early morning and it was customary during the medieval period to eat the main meal of the day during the morning. On returning to his chamber, he was dressed in a blue robe with a white hood and a piece of white silk that adorned the shoulder. Richard's brother, George, was also initiated to the Order of the Bath in St John's Chapel.

On 27 June, both brothers, as Knights of the Bath, 'being arrayed in blue gowns with hoods and tokens of white silk upon their shoulders', rode ahead of Edward IV on horseback through the streets of London to Westminster, where they resided on the night before the coronation.

Prior to his own coronation, Richard III returned to St John's Chapel to initiate seventeen Knights of the Bath on 4 July 1483.

42

Westminster Abbey

Coronation of Edward IV.

Benedictine monks founded Westminster Abbey in AD 960 and from 1066 it became the place of coronation for English sovereigns. The church that exists today was begun by Henry III in 1245. It was a place of coronation, sanctuary and burial for some of the prominent protagonists of the Wars of the Roses. On 28 June 1461, Edward IV was crowned King of England.

The reign of Edward IV began on 4 March 1461 when he claimed the throne at Westminster Abbey, but before a coronation could take place he wanted to suppress the Lancastrian army. Within six months of his father's death at Wakefield, Edward, aged 19, had defeated the House of Plantagenet at Towton and was crowned King of England. Pigello Portinari received a letter from London dated 14 April that shows the coronation of Edward IV brought hope to the people of England and confidence that the situation would improve during his reign:

> I am unable to declare how well the commons love and adore him, as if he were their God. The entire kingdom keeps holiday for the event. Thus far he appears to be a just prince, and to mean to amend and organise matters otherwise has been than has been done hitherto; so, all comfort themselves with hopes of future well-being.[65]

Edward IV had achieved his father's aspiration to claim the throne and he would become the founder of the Yorkist dynasty, which would reign for the following twenty-five years. Edward had proved himself as a general and a warrior. Edward IV was the only English king to seize the throne by force of arms, not once, but twice to regain the throne. During the day of his coronation, Edward IV elevated his brother George as Duke of Clarence and his loyal friend William Hastings to 1st Baron Hastings. Four months after his accession to the throne, Edward IV elevated Richard as Duke of Gloucester, shortly after his ninth birthday. He would also live under the guardianship of Richard Neville, Earl of Warwick.

---

65. Brown, op. cit., p.105.

Westminster Abbey. (Author's collection)

In November 1461, Edward IV opened his first parliament at Westminster and passed draconian measures against the Lancastrians. Henry IV, Henry V and Henry VI were proclaimed usurpers. Henry VI, Queen Margaret, their son Edward, alongside twelve peers and approximately 100 others who supported the Lancastrian cause and fought at Wakefield, Mortimer's Cross, St Albans and Towton, dead or alive were pronounced attainted and their estates forfeited to the Crown. Although Edward IV had taken the throne, his position was not secure while Queen Margaret was free. In April 1462, she left Henry VI in Scotland for France to seek support from Louis XI to launch a campaign against Edward IV. In exchange for French support, Calais would be returned to France if Henry VI was restored to the throne. Louis XI offered limited support, amounting to 800 French soldiers, who accompanied Queen Margaret on her return to England.

43

Execution site, Tower Hill, London

Edward IV took tough action on conspiracies against his reign.

Any indication of treachery was dealt with swiftly without trial irrespective of whether they were young or old. The elderly John de Vere, 12th Earl of Oxford, who was loyal to Henry VI, was arrested on the orders of John Tiptoft, 1st Earl of Worcester, who was appointed Constable of England by Edward IV. Without being tried, Oxford was sentenced to death because he had corresponded with Queen Margaret. On 26 February 1462, Oxford and his eldest son, Sir Aubrey de Vere, was executed with other noblemen at Tower Hill for receiving letters from the queen. Edward IV rewarded those nobles who were loyal to the Yorkists with the estates of the condemned Lancastrians.

Worcester held various positions in the king's council during the reigns of Henry VI and Edward IV. He was intelligent and cultivated, and was regarded with high esteem at home and internationally. However, Worcester was renowned as the 'butcher of England' for presiding over trials during the reign of Edward IV and ordering the executions of prominent Lancastrian noblemen with extreme brutality, having them beheaded and quartered.

Worcester suffered the same fate as those men he had condemned. Unable to escape with Edward IV during the Readeption of Henry VI in 1470, he was found in Weybridge Forest in Huntingdonshire (now Cambridgeshire) attempting to conceal himself in a tree. He was taken to London, where he was attainted on a charge of murder, treason and cruelty. Sentenced to death, he was beheaded at Tower Hill on 18 October 1470. Worcester requested that at his execution, the executioner should strike his neck with three strikes representing the Trinity. He was the only person put to death on the restoration of Henry VI to the throne. Oxford and Worcester are both commemorated on the same plaque at the Tower Hill execution site.

Tower Hill was also used as a place of execution during the reign of Henry VII. Another plaque lists three individuals who were beheaded on this site: Sir William Stanley in 1495; James Tuchet, 7th Baron Audley; and Edward Plantagenet, 17th Earl of Warwick in 1499.

Sir William Stanley was the younger brother of Thomas Stanley, Baron Stanley, who later become the 1st Earl of Derby. He was a Yorkist supporter who played an important role in the victory of Henry Tudor at Bosworth. When Henry became king, he appointed Stanley

Execution site at Tower Hill. (Author's collection)

Simon of Sudbury, Archbishop of Canterbury	1381
Sir Robert Hales	1381
Sir Simon de Burley, K.G.	1388
Richard Fitzalan, 3rd Earl of Arundel	1397
Rev. Richard Wyche, Vicar of Deptford	1440
John de Vere, 12th Earl of Oxford	1462
John Tiptoft, Earl of Worcester	1470

Above: Plaque commemorating the executions carried out during the reign of Edward IV and Henry VI. (Author's collection)

Below: Plaque listing names of individuals executed during the reign of Henry VII and Henry VIII. (Author's collection)

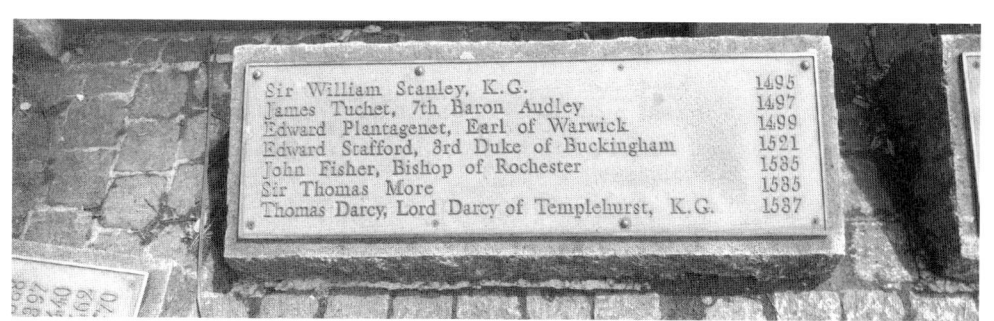

Sir William Stanley, K.G.	1495
James Tuchet, 7th Baron Audley	1497
Edward Plantagenet, Earl of Warwick	1499
Edward Stafford, 3rd Duke of Buckingham	1521
John Fisher, Bishop of Rochester	1535
Sir Thomas More	1535
Thomas Darcy, Lord Darcy of Templehurst, K.G.	1537

EXECUTION SITE, TOWER HILL, LONDON

as Chamberlain to the king's household during October 1485. He was arrested for treason and executed for his support of Perkin Warbeck in 1495. Although the evidence against him was circumstantial, Stanley confessed guilt in the hope that Henry VII would show leniency. Although the king considered clemency, he chose to carry out the death sentence because he did not want to endanger his position and encourage other attempts to usurp his throne.

James Tuchet, 7th Baron Audley, was the only Lord who joined the Cornish Rebellion that opposed the taxes and levies imposed upon them by Henry VII during 1497. Audley led the insurgents to Deptford, where they were defeated. Audley was captured, tried for treason and executed at Tower Hill on 28 June 1497.

Edward Plantagenet, 17th Earl of Warwick, was the son of George, Duke of Clarence, and Isabel Neville. Henry VII incarcerated him in the Tower of London without just cause. Four royal servants were hanged on 17 December 1489 for attempting to rescue Warwick and within a year it was claimed that the earl, aged 24, had confessed to treason and he was executed at Tower Hill on 28 December 1499.

44

Bamburgh Castle

Bastion of Lancastrian resistance.

Although Henry Percy, 3rd Earl of Northumberland, had been killed at Towton on 29 March 1461, the Northumberland castles at Alnwick, Bamburgh and Dunstanburgh remained under Lancastrian control after the coronation of Edward IV. Although the northern noblemen who owned these castles openly pledged their loyalty to the new king, they sympathised with Henry VI and opened their homes to the Lancastrians.

It would take three years to quell Lancastrian resistance in Northumberland. Queen Margaret placed responsibility to hold Bamburgh Castle upon Sir Ralph Percy and Henry Beaufort, 3rd Duke of Somerset, with 300 men. A force of Lancastrian forces including 800 French troops led by Queen Margaret set sail from Normandy and landed at Bamburgh on 25 October 1462. Margaret swiftly regained control of Northumberland. Edward IV and Warwick immediately proceeded northwards to confront her with 30,000 men. When they arrived at York on 19 November, Edward was afflicted with measles and ordered Warwick to besiege the Northumberland castle. Warwick divided his army into three as they besieged the Lancastrian garrisons at Alnwick, Bamburgh and Dunstanburgh, assigning 10,000 men to each castle. Warkworth Castle was used by Warwick as a base and he was able to ride by horse to oversee the sieges at Bamburgh, Alnwick and Dunstanburgh Castles.

The siege of Bamburgh Castle began on 11 December 1462, led by Yorkist commanders Warwick, Robert, 1st Baron Ogle, and John Neville, Baron Montagu, with 10,000 men, supported by artillery. The strategy was not to attack the castles, but starve the occupants into submission to ensure that the defences were not damaged and could be used by the Yorkists. The Lancastrians were outnumbered and this unsettled Queen Margaret, who fled once again into Scotland by sea. The journey was disastrous right from the beginning because her ship sailed into a storm and had to be abandoned, so she was compelled to continue her passage to Berwick in a smaller boat. Three accompanying ships carrying French soldiers sank with the survivors seeking safety on Holy Island, which can be seen north from Bamburgh Castle. These survivors were attacked and captured by overwhelming Yorkist forces on the shore.

As Queen Margaret sailed to Scotland, the Lancastrians still held on to Bamburgh, Alnwick and Dunstanburgh Castles. Ogle and Montagu organised the Yorkist siege of Bamburgh Castle

Aerial view of Bamburgh Castle. (Craig Duncanson/Shutterstock)

and Edward ordered Warwick to send a message promising Somerset a substantial pension if he surrendered it. Somerset agreed on the provision that ownership of the castle be passed to Sir Ralph Percy, that all lords with him had their estates restored and that the Lancastrian lives would be spared. Warwick agreed and Somerset surrendered the castle on Christmas Eve. The surrender of Dunstanburgh Castle followed on 26 December 1462. Edward IV showed them mercy by giving them their liberty and their estates were restored after swearing an oath of loyalty to him. By not executing his opponents, Edward was demonstrating that he was able to be conciliatory towards his Lancastrian foe and tried to build a peace between the houses of York and Lancaster. Somerset was now an ally of Edward IV and Sir Ralph Percy was reinstated as commander of Bamburgh and Dunstanburgh Castles.

During May 1463, Queen Margaret led Scottish and French mercenaries from Scotland across the border into England to recapture the Northumbrian castles. The trust that Edward IV placed in Sir Ralph Percy was misjudged because he reverted his allegiances to the Lancastrians and allowed Margaret's troops into Bamburgh Castle. Margaret and Henry VI followed and established it as their headquarters.

After the Lancastrian defeat at Hexham on 15 May 1464, Henry VI and Queen Margaret with their son sought sanctuary at Bamburgh Castle, together with the remnants of their defeated army, including Sir Ralph Grey, who assumed command of the garrison. It was here that she abandoned her attempts to get her husband restored to the throne and set sail with her son, Prince Edward, for Sluys in Flanders. When Margaret left Henry VI at Bamburgh it was the last time she would see him, and he fled north across the border into Scotland. For the following year he lived in hiding in various houses in northern England.

Although Henry VI and Queen Margaret had fled, the castle was still occupied by the Lancastrians, and the Earl of Warwick began a siege on 25 June 1464. London citizens had impressed Yorkist forces with their archery skills at the Second Battle of St Albans and now assisted Warwick in the assault upon Bamburgh. Sir Ralph Grey held the castle until July. An account of the siege recorded 'and then my Lord Lieutenant had ordained all the King's great-guns, that were charged, at once to shoot at the said castle: Newcastle, the king's great-gun, and London, the second gun of iron, the which betide the place, that stones of the walls flew into the sea.'[66]

The bombardment overwhelmed the defenders and enabled the Yorkists to enter the fortifications. Castles were traditionally blockaded and the occupants isolated until submission. This attack upon Bamburgh was a rare occurrence where a castle was captured after a direct assault. When a wall fell upon Grey, leaving him incapacitated, his subordinates decided to surrender the castle on the provision that they were issued a pardon from Edward IV. No dispensation was extended to Grey because once captured by Yorkist forces, he was taken to Edward IV at Pomfret Castle (Pontefract Castle) and then to Doncaster, where John Tiptoft, 1st Earl of Worcester, condemned him to death. Grey's knightly spurs were removed, heralds removed his coats of arms, which were reversed, and he was forced to wear them to his place of execution, where he was beheaded on 11 July 1464. His head was sent to London, where it was set upon a pike on London Bridge alongside those of other traitors.

---

66. Anonymous, *The Chronicles of the White Rose of York* (James Bohn, London, 1845), p.102.

45

Reading Abbey

Edward damages his relationship with Warwick.

Edward IV convened a conference at Reading Abbey during September 1464 to discuss recoining, which reduced the value of English money and meant the treasury would profit through minting new coins. He also discussed his marriage to Elizabeth Woodville (also known as Wydeville). Elizabeth was the widow of Sir John Grey, a Lancastrian knight who was killed at the Second Battle of St Albans in 1461.

Elizabeth was also the mother to two sons named Richard and Thomas Grey. Edward IV passed through Grafton Regis, near Stony Stratford, Buckinghamshire, on his journey north to suppress the rebellion in the north and it is believed that he met Elizabeth during his brief stay, during which she appealed for his help in restoring her children's inheritance and the estates that had been confiscated from her husband. Her father, Sir Richard Woodville, was an adversary and her brother, Anthony, fought against Edward, but despite the Woodvilles supporting the Lancastrians, a romantic relationship developed between Edward and Elizabeth, who was five years his senior. Soon after this initial meeting, Edward consented to her request, returned property to her family and pardoned Sir Richard and Anthony.

Edward IV and his court arrived at Stony Stratford on 30 April 1464. On the following morning, the king rode alone for 5 miles to Grafton Regis under the auspices of going hunting with Sir Richard Woodville, but instead it is believed that he married Elizabeth in secret in the presence of her mother, Jacquetta, Duchess of Bedford, a priest, two gentlewomen and a young man who sang with the priest during the service. Edward joined the court at Northampton, where it remained until 4 May before moving on to Leicester. During those four days, Edward returned to Stony Stratford to spend time with his wife and the couple kept their marriage secret. Six months later, the marriage became public knowledge at Michaelmas on 29 September at Reading Abbey when Edward IV declared to a council of peers that Elizabeth was his lawful wife and their queen.

The marriage of a sovereign was an important issue of state for it was an opportunity to marry a European princess, to establish closer alliances and to produce an heir. In Edward's case it was also a sign that he was maturing into an adult. Although Warwick's power had helped Edward attain the throne, once crowned Edward IV wanted to make his own decisions and

Reading Abbey where Edward IV convened a conference during September 1464 to discuss recoining, which reduced the value of English money and the treasury would profit from reminting new coins. He also discussed his marriage to Elizabeth Woodville. Henry I was buried in Reading Abbey in 1135. (Courtesy of Chris Wood; www.geograph.org.uk)

govern independently from his cousin. Instead, by marrying someone of his own choosing, for love, he had angered advisers such as Warwick and Lord Wenlock, who had been conducting secret negotiations with France for a suitable union with Bona of Savoy, the sister-in-law of the French king Louis XI. Securing a Yorkist alliance from this proposed marriage would ensure French support and reduce the prospect of Queen Margaret launching an invasion from France to reinstall Henry VI on the throne. In the eyes of Warwick and Wenlock, Edward had squandered this opportunity, for his marriage choice was driven by love instead of politics. Elizabeth was regarded as a commoner, and his marriage to a woman of humble lineage, which defied tradition, marked the beginning of a rift between the king and the kingmaker.

Furthermore, Warwick and Edward's brother, George, Duke of Clarence, became concerned with Edward's changing allegiances. Edward had lauded and elevated Elizabeth's family with titles, estates and prominent positions in court. After Elizabeth's coronation, Edward IV had raised her father, Sir Richard Woodville, to the title 1st Earl Rivers and appointed him Treasurer and Constable of England. He also arranged marriages for her three brothers and five sisters into wealthy families. Her brother was knighted, Sir Anthony Woodville and permitted to marry Lady Scales, who was the only daughter of Lord Scales, one of the wealthiest landowners in the country. This caused Clarence to feel resentful because he wanted to marry Lady Scales and enjoy her inheritance. Warwick felt marginalised. He had helped Edward IV in his path to seizing the throne and he was appalled by his ingratitude. Warwick and Clarence felt so threatened by the influence that the Woodvilles exerted upon the king and the subsequent dominance in court that they launched a rebellion. They would find support from other aristocratic families who resented the titles, appointments and arranged marriages that had benefited the Woodvilles, benefits that they had been denied because of Edward's bias towards his wife's family.

46

Waddington Old Hall

Capture of Henry VI.

On 15 May 1464, John Neville, Baron Montagu, Warwick's youngest brother, defeated Lancastrian forces at the Battle of Hexham, in Northumberland, and this resulted in the capture and execution of Henry Beaufort, 3rd Duke of Somerset. After the battle, Henry VI sought sanctuary in various Lancastrian safe houses in the north of England for a year. He maintained a low profile to the extent that there was speculation as to whether he was dead or alive. In July 1465 he was staying at Waddington Old Hall near Clitheroe, where he was protected by Sir Richard Tempest.

An Abingdon monk, William Cantelowe, a former protector of the king, betrayed him to the Yorkists in return for reward. Henry was apprehended on 13 July at Waddington Old Hall while he was eating dinner. Henry escaped through the grounds and tried

Waddington Old Hall. (Courtesy of Alexander P Kapp; www.geograph.org.uk)

to evade his pursuers by crossing the River Ribble across a ford known as the Hippingstones, which are close to where the Brungerley Bridge now stands. He was accompanied by a valet named Ellerton and two chaplains, Dr Beadon and Thomas Manning, the former Dean of Windsor. They were captured by Thomas Talbot, son of Sir Edmund Talbot of Bashall, and his cousin, John Talbot, assisted by Sir James Harrington, who was a prominent Yorkist living in Lancashire. Henry was placed on a horse with his leg bound to the stirrup and escorted to the Tower of London 'where King Edward ordered all possible humanity to be shown towards him, consistently with his safe custody; and, at the same time gave directions that he should be supplied with all suitable necessaries, and treated with becoming respect'.[67]

Henry arrived at the Tower of London on 25 July and would remain there as a prisoner for the following five years.

---

67. Riley, *Croyland*, op. cit., p.439.

47

Danesmoor, site of the Battle of Edgcote

Warwick and Clarence rebel against Edward IV.

During August 1469, William Herbert, 1st Earl of Pembroke, was heading from Wales with Yorkist sympathisers to join Edward IV's forces at Nottingham. Herbert had been elevated to the peerage of Pembroke by Edward IV in 1468, which originally belonged to Jasper Tudor. A rebellion in the North was erupting led by Robin of Redesdale, who was marching south to join rebel forces commanded by Warwick and George, Duke of Clarence, who were plotting against Edward. Pembroke and Redesdale would clash at Edgcote.

Cruel, unsubstantiated rumours were circulating that Edward IV was illegitimate and that his mother, Cecily, had embarked on an illicit relationship with a French soldier named Blaybourne while she was living in Rouen around 1442. These rumours may have originated from Warwick in order to discredit Edward's claim to the throne in favour of his son-in-law, George, Duke of Clarence, which would ensure that his grandson would become king in the future.

Pembroke's army engaged with Redesdale's rebel army on 26 July 1469 at Edgcote, 4 miles from Banbury. The battle took place within three small hills that formed a triangle, including Danesmoor. Pembroke suffered a setback during the night prior to the battle when he quarrelled with Humphrey Stafford, 1st Earl of Devon, about quarters and he withdrew his force of 800 archers, leaving him severely weakened and outnumbered by the rebels. Legend states that the argument was about who would spend the night with a local barmaid.

The rebels defeated Pembroke at Edgcote, where 168 Welsh noblemen died on the battlefield alongside hundreds of their men. Croyland cites 4,000 men killed. Pembroke and his brother, Richard Herbert of Coldbrook, were captured after the battle and executed on the orders of Warwick, who was in the vicinity.

Edward IV was at Olney, near Coventry, when he received news of the Yorkist defeat at Edgcote. This prompted many of his soldiers to desert him. The Archbishop of York, with a large force, took the king into his custody and took him to meet with Warwick, who received him cordially and gave an assurance that no harm would come to him. Edward IV was then taken to Kenilworth Castle. It was probable that while confined here, he witnessed the executions of

Danesmoor, site of the Battle of Edgcote. (Courtesy of David M. Jones; www.geograph.org.uk)

Richard Woodville, 1st Earl Rivers, the father of Queen Elizabeth and his father-in-law, and her brother, Sir John Woodville, within the confines of Kenilworth Castle, on Warwick's orders on 12 August 1469. Edward was then brought to Warwick Castle.

The country was in a unique position where there were two kings and both were in custody. Warwick was in a strong position and had control of the country, but he was not fully committing his full support behind Henry VI. Warwick was fearful that Yorkist sympathisers would launch an attempt to rescue Edward IV, so he was transferred to Middleham Castle. Warwick did not know what to do with Edward; after all, he was in a powerful position where he could depose him and replace him with his brother, Clarence. Eventually Warwick succumbed to pressure from Edward's supporters and he released the king after a hollow reconciliation.

48

Battle of Losecoat Field Monument

The treachery of Warwick and Clarence is revealed.

During February 1470, Lord Welles and his son, Sir Robert, aided by Sir Thomas Dymock, attacked and ransacked Gainsborough Old Hall, the home of Sir Thomas de Burgh, who was a knight of the king's household. This may have been a local disagreement, but historians have speculated that Warwick may have manipulated the situation to provoke a reaction from the king and hopefully instigate civil unrest.

The king summoned Lord Welles and Dymock to London to explain their actions, but on arrival, fearing for their own safety, they sought refuge in Westminster Abbey. Edward offered them a pardon, but it became known that Sir Robert Welles had issued proclamations for the people of Lincolnshire to resist the king and raised an army that was assembling at Horncastle.

Edward headed north to suppress this rebellion with Lord Welles and Dymock as hostages. When they reached Huntingdon, they admitted their complicity in the rebellion and Edward urged Welles to write to his son telling him to abandon the revolt and surrender to the king. The royalist army reached Stamford on 12 March, while Sir Robert Welles' men were at Empingham, 5 miles north-west. Sir Robert was prepared to engage in battle and rescue his father. Edward ordered the executions of Lord Welles and Sir Thomas Dymock on that same day. Edward also received a letter from Warwick and Clarence confirming that they would support him and were heading north.

Edward met the rebels at Empingham in Lincolnshire on 12 March 1470. The insurgent soldiers were waiting for them and shouted chants of 'Warwick' and 'Clarence', which was an indication that Edward's brother and cousin were involved and, despite their letters of support, were indeed making another attempt to seize the throne. According to the *Warkworth Chronicle*, 'the king took his host and went toward his enemies, loosed guns of his ordinance upon them, fought with them, and the commons fled away'.[68] The royalist artillery succeeded in dispersing the rebels that fled from the battlefield. As they escaped, the rebels discarded their

---

68. Warkworth, John, *A Chronicle of the first thirteen years of the reign of King Edward the Fourth* (J.B. Nichols and Son, London, 1839), p.8.

Sculpture from 2015 by Tony Rawlings to commemorate the Battle of Losecoat (Empingham) on 12 March 1470. (Courtesy of Tim Heaton; www.geograph.org.uk)

coats bearing livery emblems, some of which belonged to Clarence. It is for this reason that this engagement was known as the Battle of Losecoat Field.

Edward IV had achieved a quick victory and had captured Sir Robert Welles, who confessed under interrogation Warwick's involvement in the rebellion. Papers were also recovered from the body of a servant belonging to Clarence that confirmed Warwick and Clarence were responsible for the revolt and that their purpose was to depose Edward and install Clarence as King of England. Sir Robert Welles was beheaded for treason at Doncaster on 14 March 1470 in front of his army.

The Welles family and Dymock were used as pawns by the major instigators of this treachery, for which they paid with their lives. The Battle of Losecoat Field had revealed Warwick and Clarence's true intent and they were forced to flee to France, allowing Edward to continue to govern.

49

Angers Cathedral

Reconciliation between Queen Margaret and Warwick.

Angers Cathedral, also known as the Cathédrale Saint-Maurice d'Angers, was the scene of an unlikely reconciliation in the Wars of the Roses between Queen Margaret and Warwick. It was also where Edward, Prince of Wales, married Anne Neville, Warwick's daughter, and it was Queen Margaret's place of burial.

Unable to forge allegiances with Thomas, Baron Stanley, and his brother, John Neville, Earl of Northumberland, Warwick, accompanied by Clarence, headed to Devon, where they escaped aboard a ship to France in the hope that he could form an alliance with his nemesis, Queen Margaret. This was an unusual situation because Margaret despised Warwick and held him personally responsible for the usurpation of Henry VI.

Warwick arrived at Harfleur on 6 May 1470. In July he reached Angers, where he waited twenty days before Queen Margaret agreed to meet him. On 22 July, at Angers Cathedral, Margaret eventually met Warwick. On bended knee, he begged for forgiveness for rebelling against her husband. Maintaining the moral high ground, the conceited Margaret kept arrogant Warwick on his knee for fifteen minutes before accepting his offer of reconciliation. She pardoned him in return for his assistance in returning her husband to the English throne. To promote his own interests, he sought a union between Edward, Prince of Wales, aged 16, and his daughter, Anne Neville, aged 14. The son of Margaret of Anjou and Henry VI was obnoxious, arrogant and disturbed. Three years earlier, Giovanni Pietro Panicharolla, a Milanese ambassador in France, in a letter dated 14 February 1467, painted an unsavoury observation of his unsettling character: 'This boy, though only thirteen years of age, already talks of nothing but of cutting off heads or making war, as if he had everything in his hands or was the god of battle or the peaceful occupant of that throne.'[69]

Margaret put aside her hostility towards Warwick in favour of exacting vengeance upon the House of York and three days later the marriage pact was agreed. This would eventually make Warwick's daughter Queen of England. Clarence, who was heir to the throne, was pacified

---

69. Hinds, A.B., *Calendar of Milanese Papers: Calendar of State Papers and Manuscripts, relating to English affairs, existing in the Archives and Collections of Milan, Vol. I* (London, 1912) p.117.

Above: Angers Cathedral. (PhotoFires/Shutterstock)

Below: Interior of Angers Cathedral. (Iavan Soto Cobos/Shutterstock)

with the promise that if Anne and Edward were unable to produce an heir, he would be next in the line of succession. Margaret was reluctant to agree to the proposition, but changed her mind on the provision that Warwick successfully conquered England. On 25 July 1470, Anne was betrothed to Edward in a ceremony at Angers Cathedral, where, in the presence of King Louis XI, Warwick and Margaret swore an oath of mutual loyalty and to uphold the House of Lancaster.

On 9 September, Warwick and Clarence sailed for England in a fleet of ships supplied by King Louis. They were accompanied by Lancastrian rebels Jasper Tudor, Earl of Pembroke, and John de Vere, 13th Earl of Oxford. The rebels landed at Plymouth and Dartmouth unopposed on 13 September. By October 1470, while Edward IV was squashing a rebellion in the north, Warwick gained control of London, released Henry VI and restored him to the throne. This period would be known as the Readeption of Henry VI.

While Warwick was in England, Anne Neville remained in France and she was married to Edward in Angers Cathedral on 13 December by the General Vicar of Bayeux.

50

Compass Memorial, Purfleet Quay, King's Lynn

Edward IV departs for exile to the Netherlands during October 1470.

The Compass Memorial at Purfleet Quay commemorates Edward IV, who sailed from the quay into exile during 1470. Shaped like a compass, each segment contains a plaque that is dedicated to famous persons associated with the town's history, including Captain John Smith and Vice Admiral Lord Nelson. When Edward IV sailed from the Norfolk town, situated on the River Ouse, it was called Bishop's Lynn, a name it held until 1537, when it received its royal charter from Henry VIII and was renamed King's Lynn.

As forces led by Warwick and Clarence landed at Dartmouth in Devon on 13 September 1470 and captured London, supporters in England rallied to the Lancastrian cause. Edward IV was in Doncaster when he received the news of the impending uprising. On realising that the House of York was again under threat, Edward, accompanied by his brother, Richard, with William, Baron Hastings, and Anthony Woodville, 2nd Earl Rivers, together with their supporters, rode on horseback through the night eastwards to the northern coastline of the Wash. Embarking on small boats, they rode through a storm towards Norfolk, where they reached King's Lynn on 30 September. During the following two days they prepared to leave England for exile. Several fishing boats were berthed at King's Lynn and the Yorkist troops were crammed into them with their leaders. On 3 October, Edward fled his kingdom into exile with little money or baggage, but vowed to return. According to the Burgundian diplomat, Philippe de Commines:

> It happened by God's grace that King Edward's quarters were no great distance from the sea, and some ships that followed with provisions for his army, lay at anchor with two Dutch merchant vessels hard by. King Edward had but just time to get aboard one of them … and thus King Edward made his escape in the year 1470 by the assistance of a small vessel of his own and two Dutch merchantmen, attended only by 700 or 800 men, without any clothes but what they were to have fought in, no money in their pockets, and

Compass Memorial, Purfleet Quay, King's Lynn. (Courtesy of Dave Hitchborne; www.geograph.org.uk)

not one of them knew whither they were going. It was very surprising to see this poor king run away in this manner, and be pursued by his own servants.[70]

As the fishing fleet sailed across the North Sea towards the Netherlands, a flotilla belonging to the Hanseatic League, which had been in dispute with England for the past two years, sighted them and were in pursuit. A low tide prevented the Hanseatic ships from continuing the pursuit. Edward's ships were rescued by his friend, Louis de Bruges, Lord of Gruuthuse, Governor of Holland, who intercepted their pursuers. When the ships landed, Edward gave the master of his ship a gown as payment for the passage and promised to do more for him in the future when he was restored to the English throne.

While Edward went into exile, on 3 October 1470, Warwick and Clarence entered London, released Henry VI from the Tower of London and restored him to the throne as sovereign. Henry VI had appointed Warwick Lieutenant of England. Warwick had influence

---

70. Commines, Philippe de, *The Memoirs of Philippe de Commines* (G. Bell, London, 1877), p.191.

Compass Memorial at Purfleet Quay, King's Lynn, where Edward sailed into exile in 1470. (Courtesy of Dave Hitchborne; www.geograph.org.uk)

in court once again. Parliament was convened on 26 November 1470 and Edward IV was declared a traitor and a usurper, statutes passed during his reign were revoked and Henry VI was proclaimed King of England. His heirs would succeed him, but if Prince Edward and Anne Neville could not produce an heir, the succession would pass to George, Duke of Clarence. New coins were introduced that featured the king's head on one side and an image of St Michael on the reverse.

Queen Elizabeth and her three daughters sought sanctuary in Westminster Abbey, where she gave birth to her and Edward's first child, Edward. The birth of an heir gave hope to Yorkist supporters in England for when Edward IV would eventually return to reclaim the throne.

51

Edward IV & Richard, Duke of Gloucester (Richard III), plaque, Cromer

Edward IV returns from exile.

On Tuesday, 12 March 1471, Edward IV and his brother Richard, Duke of Gloucester (the future King Richard III), arrived at Cromer, Norfolk. This plaque commemorates their first landfall.

Louis de Bruges, Lord of Gruuthuse, visited England in 1466 and formed a strong friendship with Edward IV. He became his saviour when he arrived in Netherlands in 1470 because he supplied the Yorks with food and paid for their expenses. Edward and Richard lived in the Gruuthuse in Bruges from 13 January to 19 February 1471. After securing the finance to raise an army, they were able to plan their return to England from this building. They also arranged the loan of ships from Bruges merchantmen as well as some German vessels to transport that army to England. Eighteen vessels in total were obtained for the invasion. Their time would be spent in the Gruuthuse and Flushing, where the invasion fleet was being assembled and equipped.

Edward IV and his army were embarked aboard these vessels on 2 March 1471, but unfavourable winds and bad weather prevented them from sailing across the North Sea to the East Anglian coastline, where they expected to receive a friendly reception. They remained on board while waiting for the weather to improve. On 11 March the eighteen ships set off containing an army comprising 1,000 Englishmen and 500 Burgundians. Croyland quoted 1,500 Englishmen, Polydore Vergil confirmed that it was 'scarcely 2,000 men at arms', while Warkworth stated that it was '900 English and 300 Flemings'. Edward sailed in the Burgundian warship *Anthony* and was determined to reclaim his throne. He briefly anchored at Cromer on 12 March. One chronicler recorded that the Cardinal Thomas Bourchier, Archbishop of Canterbury, and the Bishop of Rochester, had men positioned off the Norfolk coast awaiting their arrival and went to them in boats to warn them of the state of play in Cromer. However, according to a servant of Edward IV, the knights Sir Robert Chamberlain and Sir Gilbert Debenham were sent ashore to gather intelligence to see how he would be received if he

Above: Edward IV and Richard, Duke of Gloucester, landed in England after their exile here at Cromer. (Courtesy of Spudgun67; via Wikimedia Commons)

Right: Plaque commemorating Edward and Richard's first landfall from exile at Cromer. (Courtesy of Spudgun67; via Wikimedia Commons)

EDWARD IV & RICHARD, DUKE OF GLOUCESTER (RICHARD III), PLAQUE, CROMER

landed on this stretch of coastline.[71] It was learned from local people that this part of Norfolk was strongly loyal to Henry VI and was held by representatives of John de Vere, 13th Earl of Oxford, a supporter of the House of Lancaster. Oxford's men forced the Yorkists to return to their ships and Edward IV swiftly ordered his fleet to proceed northwards.

On leaving Cromer, the fleet set sail northwards towards the Yorkshire coastline, which was regarded as a dangerous stretch unsuitable for disembarkation, but was expected to be undefended. The fleet sailed into a storm, which scattered the ships across a distance of 34 miles. On 14 March Edward IV, with 500 men,[72] landed at Ravenspur, close to Spurn Head on the north bank of the Humber Estuary. This was close to the place where Henry Bolingbroke (later Henry IV) landed when he usurped Richard II and established the House of Lancaster during 1399. Richard, Duke of Gloucester, landed 4 miles further north on that same day with 300 men. Earl Rivers and 200 men landed 14 miles from Ravenspur at Powle. Edward IV sought refuge for the night in a village 2 miles inland and he was joined by his brother and other forces during the following morning. His aim was to reach London and contend his right to the throne; however, the shortest land route was through Lincolnshire, which meant that he would be passing through a Lancastrian-supporting county. He then re-embarked his men to cross the Humber. He was refused entry into Hull, so he proceeded to York.

---

71. Anonymous, *Chronicles of the White Rose of York*, op. cit., p.37.

72. Ibid., p.37.

52

Walmgate Bar, York

Edward IV arrived in York.

Edward IV and his brother, Richard, Duke of Gloucester, passed through this entrance on returning from exile on 18 March 1471.

Walmgate Bar is the only example of a complete medieval bar, or entrance, to an English city where the barbican, portcullis and inner oak doors have survived. Consisting of three storeys, the oldest part of the structure, the stone archway, was constructed during the twelfth century. The walled barbican at the front was built during the fourteenth century and the oak doors originate from the fifteenth century. Documentation exists that suggest that tolls were collected as people passed through Walmgate Bar during 1280.

As Edward IV and Gloucester approached York from Hull, 4 miles from the city walls, they were received by Thomas Conyers (or Coniers), the City Recorder, who warned him that he would not be welcomed and refused entry into York. Edward ordered his army to establish camp, three bow shots away from York under Gloucester's command, while he continued the journey to York accompanied by fifteen men-at-arms. When they arrived at Walmgate Bar on 18 March 1471 the gates were locked and the city walls were lined by the citizens of York, who were looking down upon them. Many of them proclaimed their opposition, shouting 'Long, live king Henry.' Despite being denied access, Edward was allowed to address the townspeople from within the gates. Edward IV wore the white ostrich feather, Prince Edward's emblem, in his hat and proclaimed allegiance to Henry VI, acknowledging him as sovereign. He then spoke of his claim to the Duchy of York and that he was not interested in becoming King of England again. He also declared his intention to avenge Warwick for his disloyalty, and said the people of York shared a common distrust and dislike of Warwick. Edward and his army was given permission to stay the night in York for rest and refreshment for twelve hours, providing that they would leave. On the following day they departed York, avoiding Pontefract, which was held in strength by John Neville. King Edward IV had stripped Neville of the earldom of Northumberland and reduced him to the title Marquess of Montagu. He had then defected to join his brother, Richard Neville, Earl of Warwick. Edward IV and his brother, Richard, headed for Sandal Castle and then onto Tadcaster. From there he continued to Coventry,

Walmgate Bar, York. (Author's collection)

where he failed to entice Warwick to engage in battle, and then went to London, which was a Yorkist stronghold.

The gates of Walmgate Bar were burned by fire in 1489 during the Yorkshire Revolt led by Sir John Egremont when Henry VII introduced heavy taxation.

53

Battle of Barnet Obelisk

Death of Warwick the Kingmaker.

On 14 April 1471, Easter Sunday, Edward IV confronted his cousin, Warwick, at Barnet in Hertfordshire. It was the first experience of battle for Richard, Duke of Gloucester, who was aged 18. It was ironic that he would be using the skills of combat learned in childhood against his tutor, Warwick.

The defection of Clarence and 12,000 of his soldiers to the Yorkists strengthened Edward's position. It tipped the balance of power, which motivated Warwick into leaving Coventry and head south to secure a Lancastrian victory before Queen Margaret arrived in England. Edward IV had arrived in the capital on 11 April, where he was briefly reunited with his wife and mother at Baynard's Castle and introduced to his six-month-old son, Edward, who had been born while he was exiled. On Easter Saturday, 13 April, Edward received news that Warwick had passed through St Albans and immediately mobilised his troops. Edward kept his brother, Clarence, close so he could keep an eye upon him to ensure that he did not defect to Warwick's side. He also brought along Henry VI from the Tower of London, so that the Lancastrian king could be seen under Yorkist control in the opposing line.

Later that day the opposing sides converged upon Barnet. Richard, Duke of Gloucester, led the vanguard and, despite it being dusk, he decided to advance through the village and establish a defensive line in front of Warwick's forces, which they held during the night. Warwick was aware of their presence and ordered cannon to be fired in the Yorkist direction throughout the night, but they fired over their lines without causing any casualties. A dense fog covered and concealed both armies on the following morning, Easter Sunday. As soon as the mist was about to lift, Edward launched an attack upon the Lancastrian line. William, 1st Baron Hastings, carried the Yorkist left flank, which was overlapped by John de Vere, 13th Earl of Oxford, on the Lancastrian right flank. Troops commanded by Henry Holland, 3rd Duke of Exeter, on the Lancastrian left were outflanked by the men commanded by Gloucester. The lines commanded by Hastings, Edward IV and Gloucester were flanked by archers. Gloucester ordered his archers to fire blindly in the direction of the Lancastrian line through the mist. Cavalry was held back, ready to pursue their opponents if the Lancastrian line broke. Warwick

An obelisk commemorates the Battle of Barnet at Monken Hadley. (Courtesy of Nigel Cox; www.geograph.org.uk)

ordered trumpets to sound the alert and responded with cannon fire and arrows. Commines reported the bravery of Edward IV from second-hand sources that 'the battle was sharp and bloody: both sides fought on foot; and the king's vanguard suffered extremely in this action, and the earl's main battle advanced against his, and so near, that the king himself was engaged in person, and behaved himself as bravely as any man in either army'.[73]

As soon as the battle started, Oxford's soldiers broke through Hastings's line, forcing his troops to abandon the battlefield and retreat to London. Rumours began to spread across the capital by mid-morning that Edward had been defeated. While the left flank faltered, Gloucester realised that there was no enemy fire on his sector, capitalised on the situation and pushed forward, overwhelming Exeter's line, forcing Warwick to deploy his reserves. Gloucester was outnumbered but he persevered with the assault, finding himself at the centre of battle, wielding an axe. His situation was precarious but Gloucester held on.

Edward, with Clarence, held the central line, which became vulnerable, especially when Oxford's men returned to the battlefield after destroying his left flank. However, the line of battle had shifted 90 degrees from east to west to opposing sides fighting north to south,

---

73. Commines, op. cit., pp.200–1.

The illustration of the Battle of Barnet originates from the Ghent manuscript that chronicled the three months of Edward IV's journey from Flushing on 11 March 1471 to his visit to Canterbury on 23 May. Edward IV is depicted mounted on a horse, wearing a circlet in the left of the image, striking Richard Neville, 16th Earl of Warwick, with his lance. Edward IV did not kill Warwick at Barnet. (Ghent University Library/Public Domain)

which caused further confusion. Therefore, Oxford's men advanced straight into the line of John Neville, Marquess of Montagu, and his archers. Oxford mistakenly feared that Montagu had joined the Yorkists and fled the battlefield. Speculation arose that Montagu did defect to the Yorkists and was killed by his own men, while other reports stated that he died while fighting valiantly for Warwick.

Commines wrote of Warwick's strategy in battle that his 'custom was never to fight on foot, but when he had once led his men in the charge, he mounted on horseback himself, and if he found victory inclined to his side, he charged boldly among them; if otherwise, he took care of himself in time, and provided for his escape. But now at the importunity of his brother, the Marquis of Montagu (who was a person of great courage), he fought on foot, and sent away his horses.'[74]

Warwick had made an error of judgement in dismissing his horses. By 7.00 am, the Lancastrian line was broken and Warwick was captured and executed on the battlefield, before Edward IV could reach him to intervene. Sir John Paston, a Lancastrian knight who fought at Barnet, confirmed that over 1,000 died on both sides. Although the Lancastrians were defeated, the Yorkists suffered too, with Commines recording 1,500 killed.[75] Edward IV returned to London immediately after the battle, while Henry VI was sent to the Tower of London. The naked remains of Warwick and his brother, Montagu, were brought from Barnet to Sir Paul's Cathedral, where they were displayed for two days to prove to the citizens that they were dead and the House of Neville had ended.

---

74. Commines, op. cit., p.201.

75. Ibid., p.201.

54

Statue of Margaret of Anjou and Prince Edward, Paris

Queen Margaret's final attempt to restore Henry VI to the English throne.

Queen Margaret was the strength behind the throne of Henry VI. Where he was too weak and inept to defend his right to reign, it was Margaret who was determined and resolute in defending his crown.

Margaret was the complete opposite to her placid husband, for she was ruthless and behaved like a tyrant. Her treatment of York after his defeat at Wakefield is evident. It also demonstrated her loyalty to Henry and he was faithful to her throughout their marriage. John Blacman wrote:

> This King Henry was chaste and pure from the beginning of his days. He eschewed all licentiousness in word or deed while he was young, until he was of marriageable age, when he espoused the most noble lady, Lady Margaret … and with her and toward her he kept his marriage vow wholly and sincerely, even in the absences of the lady, which were sometimes very long: never dealing unchastely with any other woman. Neither when they lived together, did he use his wife unseemly, but with all honesty and gravity.[76]

Queen Margaret had last seen her husband in August 1463, when she left him at Bamburgh Castle. Although her husband had been restored to the throne in England between October 1470 and April 1471, Margaret remained in France with her son, Prince Edward, at the court of King Louis XI. This may have been an error of judgement, because if Edward had been present with the king, it would have strengthened their position and the Lancastrian line of succession.

During the early months of 1471, Margaret assembled a significant force to return to England in support of Warwick in his attempt to restore her husband to the throne. In England, her ally, Edmund Beaufort, 4th Duke of Somerset, left London for the West Country to muster further

---

76. James, *Blacman*, op. cit., p.29.

Statue of Margaret of Anjou, with her son, Prince Edward of Westminster, in the Jardin du Luxembourg, Paris. (Courtesy of LPLT; via Wikimedia Commons)

support to join Margaret when she landed. On 24 March, her army was assembled at Harfleur, but due to bad weather, did not set sail for England until 13 April. She was accompanied by her son, Edward. His wife, Anne Neville, landed at Weymouth the following day, while Warwick's Lancastrian forces were being annihilated at Barnet.

Margaret then proceeded from Weymouth to Cerne Abbey, where she joined forces with Edmund Beaufort, 4th Duke of Somerset, and John Courtenay, 15th Earl of Devon. They brought news of the Lancastrian defeat at Barnet and the demise of Warwick. This was a mighty setback for Margaret, who had lost her principal commander, and Anne Neville was bereaved at the loss of her father. Although disturbed by the news, the Lancastrian cause was not lost. Somerset was able to convince Margaret that Edward IV had been weakened and that the Lancastrians could reclaim the throne. Her combined force in Dorsetshire with Somerset was of significant size, Jasper Tudor, Earl of Pembroke, commanded a considerable force in Wales, and Thomas Neville (Bastard of Fauconberg) had assembled a Lancastrian fleet that was threatening to attack London. As Margaret proceeded to Exeter and then to Wells, supporters of the House of Lancaster from the south-western counties of England rallied behind her banner. In order to deceive Edward IV, she sent messengers to Shaftsbury and Salisbury to spread misinformation that she was marching towards London. If she reached Wales and secured the support of Jasper Tudor then Margaret might be in a strong position to defeat Edward and restore Henry to the throne.

55

Gupshill Manor, Tewkesbury

Queen Margaret reputedly stayed here on the eve of the Battle of Tewskesbury.

This building was constructed in 1431, although most of the original parts date from renovations made in the sixteenth and seventeenth century.

News reached Edward IV on 16 April 1471 that Margaret had landed at Weymouth two days earlier. On 24 April, Edward IV led his army from Windsor Castle westwards in an effort to pursue her army. By 30 April, Margaret had passed through Wells and had reached Bristol. Soldiers guarding the walled city of Gloucester refused to open the gates and Margaret was prevented from crossing the River Severn and entering Wales to join forces with Jasper Tudor. The next crossing of the river was at Tewkesbury and she ordered her army to continue the march to this town. Margaret arrived at Tewksbury at 4.00 pm on 3 May 1471, and after the long march, her soldiers fell to the ground exhausted and could go no further. During that evening the Lancastrian army camped south of Tewkesbury and Margaret was reputed to have stayed at Gupshill Manor, close to her soldiers. Before the Battle of Tewkesbury, Margaret and Edward, Prince of Wales, rode towards their soldiers and promised them rewards if they defeated the Yorkist army. The battle was fought just north of Gupshill Manor.

Gupshill Manor. (Courtesy of Rob Farrow, www.geograph.org.uk)

56

Ghent Manuscript, depiction of the Battle of Tewkesbury

Edward IV was not deceived by Queen Margaret's attempts into misleading him into thinking that her army was marching onto London. He wanted to intercept Margaret's Lancastrian forces in Gloucestershire to prevent her from joining forces with Jasper Tudor, Earl of Pembroke, in Wales. Tewksbury was the gateway to Wales and he had to block her passage across the River Severn.

On 4 May 1471, Richard, Duke of Gloucester, led the Yorkist vanguard to Tewkesbury. The Lancastrians were positioned on high ground south of the town with Edmund Beaumont, 4th Duke of Somerset, holding the western flank, John, 1st Baron Wenlock, in the centre with Prince Edward and John Courtenay, 15th Earl of Devon, on the eastern flank. The River Swilgate flowed on the eastern flank, while the Avon flowed into the Severn to the west. Behind them were Gaston Field and St Mary's Abbey. Gloucester attacked Somerset's line, while Edward IV advanced on the centre and William, 1st Baron Hastings, assaulted Devon's line. The Yorkist army had to pass through dykes and thick hedges before they reached the Lancastrians.

Yorkist artillery and archers targeted the Lancastrian line. If Somerset had held the line, it would have been difficult for the Yorkists to break through, but the artillery fire and arrows persuaded him to order his men to charge towards their foe instead of enduring the barrage of artillery and flight of arrows that were targeted towards them. Edward IV led his men on foot and was ready to confront the Lancastrian assault. The Yorkists were able to beat them back to their original line. Edward had also positioned a contingent of 200 spearmen in a wood west of the battlefield, so as Somerset tried to manoeuvre around upon Richard's flank, they were able to counter-attack Somerset's forces from the rear, forcing them to disperse north-west towards the Avon. Edward IV was then able to concentrate his attack upon the centre held by Lord Wenlock and Edward, Prince of Wales. Although the Lancastrians offered stout resistance, they were unable to hold the position and the line broke.

According to Holinshed, after the left flank had capitulated, Somerset returned to the Lancastrian centre and wielded an axe at Wenlock's head because he had not supported his

The Battle of Tewkesbury, as illustrated in the Ghent manuscript. King Edward IV is depicted behind the archers, knocking a Lancastrian knight from his horse, while Edward, Prince of Wales, is being killed in the foreground. (Ghent University Library/Public Domain)

charge before retreating from the battlefield to Tewkesbury Abbey. Somerset considered Wenlock's inaction as treason, but it was Somerset's decision to charge into the Yorkists that was probably the cause of the Lancastrian defeat. Somerset's brother, John Beaufort, and the Earl of Devon were slain in the battle.

57

Bloody Meadow, Tewkesbury

Site of the final rout of the Lancastrian army at the Battle of Tewkesbury.

Somerset's force was sandwiched between Edward's spearmen in a wood in the west and Richard, Duke of Gloucester's, line. They were forced to flee north-west with Gloucester in pursuit, but they ran into this meadow enclosed by trees and impenetrable hedgerows.

It was here where the fleeing Lancastrians found themselves ensnared for at the end of this field their escape was obstructed by the River Avon, which leads into the Severn. This meadow, which is long and constricted, became a killing field where retreating Lancastrians were funnelled into this restricted area and hacked to death. Some chroniclers believe that Edward, Prince of Wales, was killed on this battlefield, although there are several hypotheses about his death. Those that reached the end of this field were drowned as they crossed the Avon.

Entrance to Bloody Meadow, Tewkesbury. (Courtesy of Roy Hughes; www.geograph.org.uk)

Bloody Meadow, Tewkesbury. (Courtesy of Phillip Halling; www.geograph.org.uk)

The common soldiers who died at Tewkesbury were buried in mass graves. Evidence of such burials was uncovered in 1860 during sewerage excavations in Lower Lode Lane. This skirts the western edge of Bloody Meadow, where human bones were discovered and assumed to have been soldiers who drowned in the nearby Avon.

Gloucester's actions became decisive and were pivotal in crushing the Lancastrians. After supressing Somerset, Gloucester led his men eastwards to attack Wenlock's right flank as his brother Edward IV was attacking from the south.

58

Burial site of Prince Edward, Tewkesbury Abbey

The Prince of Wales was killed at the Battle of Tewkesbury.

It was Edward, Prince of Wales' first combat experience at Tewkesbury, where he fought alongside the Lancastrian central line commanded by Wenlock. Aged 17, he was the only heir apparent to the English throne to die in battle.

There were various contradictory accounts about how Edward was killed at Tewkesbury. Warkworth confirmed that 'the most part of the people fled away from the prince, by which the field was lost in hire party and there was slain in the field, Prince Edward which cried for succour from his brother-in-law, the Duke of Clarence'.[77]

According to *Fabyan's Chronicle*, Prince Edward was 'brought unto the king. After the king had questioned with the said sir, Edward, and he had answered unto him contrary to his pleasure, he then struck him with his gauntlet upon his face, after which stroke so by him received, he was by the king's servants slain.'[78]

Hall recorded that Prince Edward was captured on the battlefield by Sir Richard Croftes. Hall wrote:

> after the field ended, King Edward made a proclamation that who so ever could bring Prince Edward to him slain or dead, should have an annuity during his life, and the prince's life to be saved, Sir Richard Croftes, a wise and valiant knight … brought forth his prisoner prince Edward, being a goodly feminine and well featured young gentleman, whom when king Edward had well advised, he demanded of him, how he durst so presumptuously enter in to his realm with banner displayed. The prince being bold of stomach and of a good courage answered saying, to recover my father's kingdom and inheritance, from his father and grandfather to him, after him to me, lineally descended. At which words king Edward said nothing … but some say struck him with his gauntlet,

---

77. Warkworth, op. cit., p.18.

78. Fabyan, Robert, *The New Chronicles of England and France* (Longman, London, 1811) p.662.

Plaque commemorating the resting place of Edward, Prince of Wales. (Courtesy of Phillip Halling; www.geograph.org.uk)

whom incontinent, they that stood about George, Duke of Clarence, Richard, Duke of Gloucester, Thomas Marques Dorset and William Lord Hastings, suddenly murdered.[79]

It was certain that Prince Edward died a violent death and his demise extinguished any hope that the House of Lancaster would continue to reign. There is conjecture caused by conflicting accounts as to where the remains of the prince were buried. It is believed that he was buried in the choir of Tewkesbury Abbey, but Tudor propaganda speculated that he was placed in a mass grave with other soldiers. There was once a marble slab at the entrance to the choir, which was removed towards the end of the eighteenth century. During this renovation work, the remains of a male youth were found by the pulpitum step at the west entrance to the monk's choir, which was in front of the current choir. A brass memorial plaque was positioned on the floor and the following words in Latin were inscribed:

> That the memory of Edward, Prince of Wales, brutally murdered after the battle fought in the fields close by, perish not utterly, the piety of the people of Tewkesbury had this memorial laid down in 1796.

Further renovation work took place during the 1870s, when another grave was found by the north-west pier of the tower with a coffin that bore the Prince of Wales helm carved upon it.

---

79. Hall, op. cit., p.301.

The Yorkist Sun is positioned on the ceiling directly above the choir in Tewkesbury Abbey where Prince Edward was buried. (Courtesy of Bs0u10e01; via Wikimedia Commons)

The chancel floor was re-laid and the original plaque dedicated to the prince was replaced with a diamond-shaped plaque, which is situated in front of the alter. The plaque is inscribed in Latin and states:

> Here lies Edward, Prince of Wales, cruelly slain whilst but a youth, anno Domini 1471, May 4th. Alas the savagery of men. Thou art the sole light of thy mother, the last hope of thy race.

The diamond plaque dedicated to the last Lancastrian heir is positioned beneath the gilded Yorkist Sun in Splendour, motif of Edward IV, which adorns the choir ceiling. The plaque installed in 1796 was relocated to the south transept.

59

Tewkesbury Abbey

Lancastrian lords seek sanctuary within the abbey.

The Lancastrian line was south of Tewkesbury Abbey and it is speculated that Queen Margaret observed the battle from this vantage point. As soon as the Yorkists broke through, defeated Lancastrian nobleman, who were fearful of their fate, escaped from the field of battle and sought sanctuary within the abbey.

Philippe de Commines, the Burgundian diplomat, met Edward IV in 1470 and recalled: 'King Edward told me, that in all the battles which he had gained, his way was, when the victory was on his side, to mount on horseback, and cry out to save the common soldiers, and put the gentlemen to the sword, by which means none, or very few of them escaped.'[80]

At Tewkesbury, Edward IV followed the defeated Lancastrian commanders with sword drawn to the doors of the abbey. The abbot appealed to him to respect the religious house, to which Edward complied and offered a pardon to any Lancastrian soldier taking refuge, except for their leaders. The Yorkist victors besieged the abbey for two days until Edward IV ordered the abbot to hand over these men into his custody. On 6 May 1471, about a dozen men were dragged out of the abbey, including Edmund Beaufort, 4th Duke of Somerset, Sir Hugh Courtenay and Sir John Langstrother, who were taken to the marketplace in the town. There they were tried before a summary tribunal presided over by John Mowbray, 4th Duke of Norfolk, Marshal of England, and Richard, Duke of Gloucester, in his role as Constable of England. These men had rebelled against the king and a guilty verdict was undisputable. After the prisoners were found guilty they were immediately executed in the marketplace at Tewkesbury. Somerset's family had suffered during the Wars of the Roses, because his father Edmund was slain in battle at St Albans in 1455 and his brother, Henry, was captured after the Battle of Hexham and beheaded in 1464. He was the last direct male Beaufort descendant of John of Gaunt. Margaret Beaufort was Somerset's only surviving relative, and her son, Henry Tudor, would be the future Henry VII.

---

80. Commines, op. cit., p.192.

Edward IV could have avenged the fate of his father, brother and uncle after the Battle of Wakefield, eleven years previously, when their decapitated heads were impaled on spikes and placed on the battlements of Micklegate Bar in York. However, after the Battle of Tewkesbury, the corpses of the executed Lancastrian lords were not dismembered or displayed, but instead accorded a decent burial. Their families were given the choice of where they should be buried, and most chose burial within Tewkesbury Abbey. Somerset was buried in St James's Chapel. Edward's respectful treatment of the executed traitors may have been a political decision to end family feuds and settle tensions in the kingdom.

The Battle of Tewkesbury was the last Yorkist victory in the Wars of the Roses and it was due to the leadership, courage and determination of Edward IV. He was not beholden to anyone for his own restoration except for the men that he commanded. Three days after the battle, Queen Margaret and Anne Neville, Princess of Wales, were captured in a convent close to Tewskesbury. Margaret's fiery defiance had been extinguished by the death of her only son and she was a shadow of her former self. Although Edward had defeated the Lancastrian rebellion in the west, Thomas Neville, the Bastard of Fauconberg, the illegitimate son of the Earl of Kent, had sailed with a detachment of Lancastrian supporters from the Calais garrison and had landed in Sandwich. There he was about to launch a further Lancastrian assault upon

Tewkesbury Abbey. (Courtesy of Saffron Blaze; via Wikimedia Commons)

Above: 'Sanctuary (Edward IV and Lancastrian Fugitives at Tewkesbury Abbey)' by Richard Burchett. (Guildhall Art Gallery/Public Domain)

Left: The Ghent manuscript shows Edward IV, on the left, watching the execution of the Lancastrian commanders at Tewkesbury. Edmund Beaufort, 4th Duke of Somerset, is shown with his head over the block, just as the axe strikes, while other Lancastrian prisoners wait for their turn to receive the same punishment. (Ghent University Library/Public Domain)

London. Edward was unaware of this insurgency and proceeded to Coventry in order to secure his position in the Midlands.

Tewkesbury would feature once again in the story of the Wars of the Roses when, after his suspicious death in the Tower of London in 1478, George, Duke of Clarence, was buried in Tewkesbury Abbey in the vault in which his wife, Isabel Neville, was buried when she died in 1476.

60

Model of the medieval London Bridge

Remnants of Lancastrian resistance in an attempt to use London Bridge to enter the city to rescue Henry VI from captivity in the Tower of London.

The old medieval bridge that spanned the River Thames during the Wars of the Roses was built between 1176 and 1209, and was 30 yards east of the current bridge. The Church of St Magnus the Martyr was at the northern end of the bridge, where a model of the bridge is on display. It was the scene of two battles fought during the Wars of the Roses: the revolt led by Jack Cade in 1450 and that started by the actions of Thomas Neville, the Bastard of Fauconberg (cousin of Warwick the Kingmaker), during 1471.

London Bridge was regarded as one of the wonders of the world during the medieval period. It was magnificent and longer than the Rialto Bridge in Venice and the Ponte Vecchio in Florence. London Bridge was supported by twenty piers built to reinforce nineteen arches. Wooden piles made of elm were driven into the riverbed in an elliptical shape, and masonry was constructed above them. Houses and shops were built upon the bridge. There was a chapel dedicated to St Thomas à Becket built in the middle of the bridge. On the approach from Southwark, pedestrians would cross two arches before reaching a stone gate, which was fortified. After crossing a further four arches, pedestrians would reach another strongly fortified tower, where there was a drawbridge that could be raised for tall ships. It was upon the battlements on this fortification that the heads of traitors were stuck on pikes and displayed as a warning to Londoners and visitors of the consequences of treachery. These included a lawyer of the Temple and eight London merchants who were executed for carrying bowstrings and pointed arrows while attempting to join Richard Neville, 16th Earl of Warwick, in Calais during 1460. On 2 July 1460, when Warwick led his troops from Sandwich, thirteen of his 30,000 followers were crushed to death on this bridge as they entered London due to overcrowding. They were laden down by the heavy armour that they wore and were unable to get up from the ground as too many people converged upon the bridge.

While Edward IV was pursuing Queen Margaret's army at Tewkesbury in 1471, the last remaining Lancastrian force raised by Thomas Neville, the Bastard of Fauconberg, comprising

A part of the model of the Old London Bridge that was created by David T. Aggett, a liveryman of The Worshipful Company of Plumbers, in 1987. It depicts the bridge as it would have appeared around 1400. The heads of traitors who had been executed were placed upon pikes on the battlements of the gatehouse to London Bridge, which also included a drawbridge that can be seen here on the left. (Author's collection)

A Blue Plaque at St Magnus the Martyr Church. The medieval London Bridge stood about 30 yards east of where the current bridge is positioned. The churchyard of St Magnus the Martyr formed part of the roadway approach to the bridge from the north. The model of the bridge can be viewed inside this church. (Author's collection)

Masonry from the medieval Old London Bridge on display outside St Magnus the Martyr Church. (Author's collection)

of mariners and mercenaries loyal to Warwick from Kent were mustering in the county. Warwick had appointed his cousin, Fauconberg, as Vice Admiral and was able to use the fleet that he commanded in the English Channel to sail up the River Thames to besiege London. On 11 May 1471, Fauconberg demanded the release of Henry VI from the Tower of London. Edward IV's wife, Queen Elizabeth, and son, Prince Edward, were also in the Tower of London, under the protection of her brother, Anthony, 2nd Earl of Rivers. On 12 May 1471, a contingent attacked the city walls at Bishopsgate and Aldgate while mariners in ships attacked the old medieval London Bridge, where Croyland confirmed that:

> they made furious assaults, and laid waste everything with sword and fire, in order, by some means or other to effect an entrance. The vestiges of their misdeeds are even yet to be seen upon the said bridge, as they burned all the houses which lay between the drawbridge and the outer gate, that looks towards the High Street of Southwark, and which had been built at vast expense.[81]

---

81. Riley, *Croyland*, op. cit., p.467.

Old London Bridge. (Author's collection)

Fauconberg placed artillery along the southern bank of the Thames and bombarded the capital. The inhabitants of the capital held their ground and resisted the barrage with their own artillery. Fauconberg also attempted to attack the drawbridge from one of his ships using gunpowder, fire and straw. The gates and thirteen houses on the bridge were destroyed by fire. Unable to enter the City of London across London Bridge, the Lancastrians persevered in trying to break through the entrance at Bishopsgate, until Earl Rivers led a cavalry charge from the Tower of London and supressed their attack. When an advanced contingent belonging to Edward IV reached the city, Fauconberg abandoned the siege and bolted for Sandwich, where his fleet was waiting to evacuate him.

Edward IV entered London on 21 May 1471 in triumph, bestowing the honour upon his brother, Richard, to lead the victorious Yorkist troops. William, 1st Baron Hastings, and Clarence were also in the process with the defeated and demoralised Queen Margaret in a chariot. Edward IV rewarded the mayor, the recorder and several aldermen who had distinguished themselves during the defence of London with knighthoods. Fauconberg's ship's did not leave Sandwich and surrendered to Richard, Duke of Gloucester. When Fauconberg tried to escape by sea, he was captured at Southampton and taken to Middleham Castle, where he was beheaded on 22 September 1471. His head was placed on a spike set upon London Bridge, facing Kent, on 27 September.

61

The King's Private Chapel, the Wakefield Tower

Henry VI died here on 21 May 1471.

The Wakefield Tower was initially called the Blundeville Tower and it is one of the oldest parts of the medieval palace at the Tower of London. Its construction was ordered by Henry III in 1220 to form a new riverside palace for when the king and queen resided at the fortress. During the Wars of the Roses, the Wakefield Tower was used as a prison to incarcerate Henry VI for six years from 1465 until 1471, except when Edward IV was overthrown and briefly exiled in Flanders.

After Tewkesbury, Edward IV returned to London again in triumph on 21 May 1471, accompanied by his brothers and the captured Margaret of Anjou. During that night in the Tower of London, Henry VI went to the chapel in the Wakefield Tower to pray. John Blacman wrote that:

> in church or chapel he was never pleased to sit upon a seat or to walk to and fro as do men of the world, but always with bare head, at least while the divine office was being celebrated, and hardly ever raising his royal person, kneeling one may say continuously before his book, with eyes and hands upturned, he was at pains to utter with the celebrant (but with the inward voice) the mass prayers, epistles, and gospels.[82]

Henry VI died in the chapel in the Wakefield Tower under mysterious circumstances. Richard, Duke of Gloucester, visited the captive king to inform him about the defeat of the Lancastrian army at Tewkesbury, the capture of his wife, Margaret of Anjou, and the death of his only son, Edward, Prince of Wales. The official Yorkist version of events stated that Henry died of grief, that he 'toke it so great, ire and indignation, that of pure displeasure and melancholy he died'.[83]

Friends of Henry VI and Lancastrian sympathisers claimed that he was murdered, stabbed to death while he was praying in this chapel within the Wakefield Tower. The fifteenth-century

---

82. James, *Blacman*, op. cit., p.28.

83. Bruce, John, *History of the Arrival of Edward IV* (Camden Society, London, 1838), p.38.

The Wakefield Tower (left), where Henry VI was incarcerated within the Tower of London. (Author's collection)

chronicler John Warkworth recorded that: 'the same night that King Edward came to London, King Henry, being inward in prison in the Tower of London, was put to death, the twenty first day of May, on a Tuesday night between eleven and twelve of the clock: being then at the Tower, the Duke of Gloucester, brother to King Edward, and many other'.[84]

The *Croyland Chronicle* intimated that Edward IV was complicit in the suspicious death. 'King Henry VI was found dead in the Tower of London; may God spare and grant time for repentance to the person, whoever he was, who thus dared to lay sacrilegious hands upon the Lord's anointed! Hence it is that he who perpetuated this has justly earned the title of traitor.'[85]

According to a letter written by Sforza de Bettini to the Duke of Milan on 17 June 1471:

> King Edward has not chosen any longer to have custody of King Henry, although he is as it were guiltless and a personage whose affairs are not such as to cause much suspicion. The prince, his son, and the Earl of Warwick have perished. All his most powerful

84. Warkworth, op. cit., p.21.

85. Riley, *Croyland*, op. cit., p.468.

The King's Private Chapel, within the Wakefield Chapel, where Henry VI was reputed to have been killed. (Author's collection)

adherents have shared the same fate, or are in the Tower of London, where he himself is a prisoner. King Edward has had him put to death secretly ... He has in short chosen to crush the seed.[86]

It was speculated that Edward IV ordered the death of Henry VI and that Richard, in his capacity as Constable of England, conveyed the order to Lord Dudley, the Constable of the Tower of London. Fabyan affirmed that 'he was struck with a dagger by the hands of the Duke of Gloucester'.[87] Commines heard rumours that Gloucester carried out the murder, because he wrote that 'this King Henry was a very ignorant prince and almost an idiot (if what was told me be true) after the battle was over, the Duke of Gloucester slew this poor King Henry with his own hand, or caused him to be carried into some private place, and stood by while he was killed'.[88]

Edward IV spent two days in London before proceeding to Sandwich to pursue Fauconberg. Holinshed stated that Henry VI was alive up until 25 May 1471, which contradicts the 21 May

---

86. Brown, op. cit., p.128.

87. Anonymous, *Chronicles of the White Rose of York*, p.94.

88. Commines, op. cit., p.201.

Plaque stating that Henry VI died in the King's Private Chapel. (Author's collection)

date on the plaque in the King's Chapel in the Wakefield Tower. If this was the case, then Richard is exonerated of blame or responsibility for the death of Henry VI for he went into Kent ahead of his brother. However, it is doubtful that Henry VI would have been murdered by Gloucester with his own hands and become the victim of Edward IV's cruelty.

Henry was residing in the Wakefield Tower under the custody of William Sayer and Robert Radcliff, who received money to cover the wages of thirty-six attendants, food and various living expenses, so there were other people close to him at the time of his demise.

Whatever the actual circumstances of Henry's death, his passing came at a convenient time for Edward IV, because he was the figurehead of the Lancastrian cause and now that he was removed, and his son and heir, Edward, Prince of Wales, had been killed at Tewkesbury, there was no one who could replace that void, which would strengthen the Yorkists' hold on the crown.

Queen Margaret was brought to the Tower of London as a prisoner during that same evening and Henry was dead before she had arrived. She was told of his death days later and was devastated. Her cries of despair could be heard on the streets outside the Tower of London. Edward IV could have avenged his father's death at the hands of Margaret, but he treated her with greater leniency than she had shown to his father in York after the Battle of Wakefield. Edward kept her captive in the custody of Alice de la Pole, widow of William de la Pole, 1st Duke of Suffolk. He was the former Chamberlain to Henry VI, who had arranged his marriage to Margaret. Alice once served Margaret as a lady in waiting. In 1475 Margaret was ransomed for 50,000 crowns and permitted to return to her native France in accordance with a treaty negotiated with King Louis XI. She died aged 52 at Dampierre-sur-Loire in Anjou on 25 August 1482.

A plaque is dedicated to Henry VI in the chapel of the Wakefield Tower, which states 'By tradition, Henry VI died here, May 21 1471'. The Ceremony of the Lilies and the Roses has taken place in this chapel every year on the evening of 21 May, the day of his death, since 1923, to remember his passing. It is attended by representatives from King's College, Cambridge, and Eton College, which were founded by this ill-fated king.

62

Engraving of Henry VI

Henry VI laid to rest.

Henry VI was originally buried in Chertsey Abbey in 1471, but his remains were transferred to St George's Chapel at Windsor Castle on the orders of Richard III in 1484.

During the morning after his death, 22 May 1471, Ascension Day, the body of Henry VI was placed on a bier and taken through the streets of London to St Paul's Cathedral, where it was displayed to prove to the citizens that he was dead. The corpse was still bleeding at the cathedral which is evidence to suggest that his death was violent. According to Warkworth, 'his face was open so every man might see him, and in his lying he bleed on the pavement there.'[89]

The corpse continued to bleed as Henry VI was later taken to Blackfriars. His remains were transported by boat along the Thames to Chertsey, where they were interred at Chertsey Abbey. English soldiers stationed at Calais were brought to London to guard the body during its journey.

On 12 August 1484, Richard III ordered that the remains of Henry VI be removed from his obscure grave at Chertsey Abbey for reinterment in St George's Chapel, Windsor, which he paid for from his own funds. Some historians believed that he murdered Henry VI or was present when he was mercilessly killed in the Wakefield Tower, but this action could be seen as exonerating him. Henry VI had been revered as a saint and Richard's motives in transferring his body may have been driven by his own religious faith, as an act of decency. He may have also felt that Henry had been wronged and that Edward IV may have sanctioned his killing, of which Richard may have disapproved as he did the death of their brother, George, Duke of Clarence.

During November 1910, the bones of Henry VI were exhumed. They had been encased in a wooden chest, within a lead casket. The remains were examined and were confirmed to be of a man who was strong and measured approximately 6ft tall. Some bones, including the right arm, were missing, probably due to the fact that he was buried in earth at Chertsey and these were lost when they were exhumed to be transferred to St George's Chapel. The examination

---

89. Warkworth, op. cit., p.21.

Engraving of Henry VI. (Wellcome Collection)

also revealed the remaining hair on his skull was darker than the rest and was matted with blood, indicating that he had a violent death. The remains of Henry VI were wrapped in white silk and placed in a new oaken box, which were then enclosed in the renovated lead casket before being returned to the vault.

63

Stained glass window commemorating marriage of Richard, Duke of Gloucester, and Anne Neville

This stained glass window commemorating the event is displayed at Cardiff Castle.

Richard married Anne Neville, daughter of the Earl of Warwick, during the spring of 1472 in St Stephen's Chapel, in the Palace of Westminster.

After the Yorkist victory at Tewkesbury, Anne Neville was captured and placed under the custody of George, Duke of Clarence. Richard, Duke of Gloucester, would have known the widowed Anne from childhood and they would have been friends. Although Gloucester was her husband's opponent at Tewkesbury, when he returned from Sandwich, he sought her hand in marriage. Clarence was married to Anne's sister, Isabel Neville, and was not enthralled by the prospect of his brother marrying Anne because he would have to share the inheritance of the sisters that had been left by Warwick the Kingmaker, which he hoped to claim in its entirety in right on behalf of his wife. In order to obstruct his brother, according

Stained glass window at Cardiff Castle commemorating marriage of Richard, Duke of Gloucester, and Anne Neville. (Courtesy of VeteranMP; via Wikimedia Commons)

to Croyland, Clarence hid Anne in London, but Gloucester found her disguised as a cook's maid. Disregarding the fact that Warwick's widow was still alive and should have been the beneficiary to her husband's estate, a bitter row erupted between Clarence and Gloucester over the inheritance. According to the *Croyland Chronicle* 'such violent dissensions arose between the brothers'.[90] Edward IV acted as mediator in the dispute and Gloucester relinquished claim to Warwick's titles so that he could marry Anne. After distinguishing himself in battle at Barnet and Tewkesbury, Gloucester had impressed his brother, Edward, who appointed him as his chief general and his trusted advisor.

---

90. Riley, *Croyland*, op. cit., p.468.

64

Church of St Mary and All Saints, Fotheringhay

Burial place of the brother and parents of Edward IV and Richard III.

The majestic tower and lantern of the Church of St Mary and All Saints dominates the skyline around the village of Fotheringhay in Northamptonshire. It is plausible that Richard III was baptised here shortly after his birth during October 1452.

The bodies of Richard Plantagenet, 3rd Duke of York, and Edmund, Earl of Rutland, were originally buried at Pontefract. In 1476, Edward IV ordered that their remains be exhumed and brought to the Church of St Mary and All Saints, Fotheringhay, which was close to the castle. Thomas Whiting, the Chester Herald, witnessed the reinterment and recorded the following details:

> On 24 July, the bodies were exhumed, that of the duke garbed in ermine furred mantle and cap of maintenance, covered with a cloth of gold, lay in state on a hearse blazing with candles, guarded by an angel of silver bearing a crown of gold as a reminder that by right the duke had been King. On the journey, Richard, Duke of Gloucester, with other lords and officers at arms, all dressed in mourning, following the funeral chariot, drawn by six horses, with trappings of black, charged with the arms of France and England and proceeded by a knight bearing the banner of the ducal arms. Each night they rested – Doncaster, Blythe, Tuxford le Clay, Newark, Grantham, Stamford and finally Fotheringhay Church was reached on 29 July, where members of the college and other ecclesiastics went forth to meet the cortege. At the entrance to the churchyard, King Edward IV waited, together with the Duke of Clarence, the Marquis of Dorset, Earl Rivers, Lord Hastings and other noblemen. Upon the arrival the king made obeisance to the body right humbly and put his hand on the body and kissed it, crying all the time.
>
> The procession moved into the church where two hearses were waiting, one in the choir for the body of the duke and the other in the Lady Chapel for that of the Earl, and after the king had retired to his closet and the princes and officers of arms had stationed themselves around the hearse, masses were sung and the King's Chamberlain

offered for him seven pieces of cloth of gold which were laid in a cross on the body. The next day three masses were sung, the Bishop of Lincoln preached a very noble sermon and offerings were made by the Duke of Gloucester and the other Lords. There were presented the Duke of York's coat of arms, his shield. His sword, his helmet and his coarser on which rode Lord Ferrers in full armour, holding in his hand an axe reversed. When the funeral was over, the people were admitted into the church and it is said that before the coffins were placed on the vault which had been built under the Chancel, five thousand people came to receive the alms, while four times that number partook of the dinner, served partly in the castle and partly in the King's tents and pavilions. There they partook of so many good things that the bills for it amounted to more than three hundred pounds – more than the cost of the church built only thirty years before.[91]

Contrary to Whiting's testimony, Richard, 3rd Duke of York, and Edmund, Earl of Rutland, were initially buried in the grounds of the church. In 1495, the remains of Cecily Neville, Duchess of York, were brought to Fotheringhay to be buried alongside her husband and son. In 1539 the church was surrendered to the Crown during the reformation and the graves were desecrated. In 1548 it was granted to John Dudley, 1st Earl of Northumberland, who stripped the lead from the church roof and dismantled adjacent buildings. In 1566, Queen Elizabeth I visited Fotheringhay Church and was dismayed that the graves of the royal dukes had been desecrated. Although their descendants were from the House of York, the opponents of Henry Tudor, she ordered that their remains be exhumed and reinterred inside the church, together with a monument. On the left side of the altar is the monument and tomb of

Church of St Mary and All Saints, Fotheringhay. (Harvey Fryer/Shutterstock)

91. Information panel, Church of St Mary and All Saints, Fotheringhay.

The Elizabethan tomb of the brother and parents of Edward IV and Richard III. (Author's collection)

Richard, Cecily and Edmund, the parents and brother to Edward IV and Richard III. The monument and tomb on the right side of the altar is dedicated to Edward, 2nd Duke of York, who was killed at the Battle of Agincourt in 1415.

CHURCH OF ST MARY AND ALL SAINTS, FOTHERINGHAY

65

Yorkist Heraldry

The Church of St Mary and All Saints, Fotheringhay, is a shrine to the House of York.

As well as being the burial place of Richard, Duke of York, and his wife, Cecily, the church is rich in Yorkist symbolism and iconography.

The Yorkist emblem of the Falcon and Fetterlock decorates the fan vault ceiling of the Church of St Mary and All Saints, Fotheringhay. Falcons were valued by medieval nobleman for their alertness and hunting ability. Edward III first used the falcon for

The Yorkist Badge of the Falcon and Fetterlock. (Author's collection)

Above left: The pulpit donated by Edward IV to St Mary's Church, Fotheringhay, is adorned with Yorkist heraldic symbolism. (Author's collection)

Above right: The rear panel of the pulpit contains the royal arms of Edward IV, flanked by the white boar for Richard of Gloucester and the black bull representing George of Clarence. England is represented by the three lions in the second and third quarters and France is signified by three fleur-de-lys in the first and fourth quarters. (Author's collection)

his badge. Edmund Langley, 1st Duke of York, adopted the emblem of a falcon, representing the Plantagenets, inside a golden fetterlock. A fetterlock is a shackle that was traditionally used in heraldry and often appeared as a padlock. Edward IV also used the emblem, but the fetterlock is slightly open to signify his struggle to attain the throne by forcing the lock. Richard III would use the falcon as a heraldic emblem on his shield.

Edward IV donated the ornately decorated pulpit that stands on a pedestal adjacent to the first pier of the north arcade within the church. The pulpit is surmounted by a hexagonal, fan-vaulted canopy and on the rear panel are the royal arms of Edward IV, flanked by the white boar for Richard of Gloucester and the black bull representing George of Clarence. England is represented by the three lions in the second and third quarters, and France is signified by three fleur-de-lys in the first and fourth quarters.

The Chapel of All Souls (York Chapel) contains the York Window, a large stained-glass window that was presented by the Richard III Society in 1975. In the centre from top to bottom are the Royal Arms of Richard III; his badge of the white boar; and the arms of Richard Neville, Earl of Warwick, the father of Anne Neville, who was the wife of Richard III. In the left column, top to bottom, are the arms of Edmund, 1st Duke of York; the arms of

YORKIST HERALDRY

The York Window, the Church of St Mary and All Saints, Fotheringhay. (Author's collection)

Edward, 2nd Duke of York, with the arms of his wife, Philippa; and the Yorkist badge of the falcon and fetterlock. In the right column, from top to bottom, are the arms of the Earl of Cambridge, brother to Edward, 2nd Duke of York; the arms of Richard, 3rd Duke of York, and his wife, Cecily Neville; and at the bottom the white lion of Mortimer.

66

Bowyer Tower

The execution of George, Duke of Clarence, by drowning in a butt of malmsey wine in the Tower of London.

Throughout his reign, Edward IV had to fight to consolidate his position as King of England, even within his own family. His brother, George, Duke of Clarence, was ambitious and had aspirations to succeed him.

On 3 April 1471, after siding with Warwick, Clarence switched sides and reconciled with his brother, Edward IV. When Gloucester married Anne Neville, he had a rightful claim to her family estate, which caused friction with his brother, Clarence, who was married to her sister, Isabel, and wanted it all. During 1472 to 1474, the division of the estates belonging to Richard Neville, 16th Earl of Warwick, between Clarence and Gloucester caused a family feud that could have resulted in violence had it not been for Edward IV's intervention to apportion the wealth fairly between the brothers. Although armed confrontation was averted, Clarence still remained unsatisfied with his allocation.

Isabel died aged 25 in 1476, leaving Clarence a widower, and during the following year he requested to marry on two occasions. However, both requests were declined by the king and this caused further tension between the brothers. Clarence was a volatile, dangerous man, and a threat to the king and the stability of the nation if his behaviour was not managed. The king therefore ordered the arrest of Clarence in June 1477 and he was brought to the Tower of London. Initially he was lodged in the comfortable chambers of the White Tower, but he was later transferred to the Bowyer Tower. During the beginning of 1478 Clarence was charged by Parliament with treason relating to various previous misdemeanours. Henry Stafford, 2nd Duke of Buckingham, was assigned High Steward of England to judge the case and on 7 February he found Clarence guilty and sentenced him to death. To avoid a public execution, the sentence was conducted in private within the confines of the Tower of London. On 18 February, Clarence was executed. His death was reported on that date, but no explanation as to how he was executed was offered. It was left to conjecture and rumour. According to other chroniclers, he was actually executed on 8 March.[92] It was speculated that

---

92. Bayley, op.cit., p.48.

Bowyer Tower is the circular tower in the centre of the photograph. (Author's collection)

he was killed by drowning in a butt of Malmsey wine. His remains were buried in Tewkesbury Abbey.

Although Edward had authorised the execution, he regretted doing so. Richard, Duke of Gloucester, was profoundly affected by grief at the loss of his brother. The Italian cleric Dominic Mancini testified that Richard was:

> overcome with grief for his brother ... Thenceforth Richard came very rarely to court. He kept himself within his own lands and set out to acquire the loyalty of his people through favours and justice. The good reputation of his private life and public activities powerfully attracted the esteem of strangers.[93]

---

93. Cheetham, Anthony, *Life & Times of Richard III* (Weidenfeld and Nicolson Limited, 1972), p.91.

67

Engraving of Edward IV

Restoration of strong leadership on the English throne.

Edward IV was the only English sovereign to have gained the throne through force on two occasions. He returned from exile in 1471 with a handful of men and was able to obtain support, build an army and defeat his foe in two battles and reclaim the crown within three months.

After the Yorkist victory at Tewkesbury and the death of Henry VI during 1471, Edward IV was able to reign freely for the following twelve years. He was able to provide strong government, maintain the royal treasury and restore stability to a nation that had been in turmoil during the previous decades. He focused on strengthening the judiciary system, and encouraged the rise of new nobility to help reduce the conflicts of the old nobility. He maintained low revenue and expenditure of government. Edward IV favoured peaceful diplomacy at the forefront of his foreign policy to avoid costly wars and would encourage trade and commerce to flourish.

Edward IV was handsome, charismatic, affable and popular among his subjects. When his skeleton was analysed during 1789, it was discovered that he would have been 6ft 4in tall and would have towered over his subjects. Long brown hair that had fallen from his skull was found, a lock of which is preserved in the Ashmolean Museum, Oxford. His wife, Queen Elizabeth, bore him ten children including two sons, Edward and Richard, which helped to secure the dynasty of the House of York. He enjoyed physical sports such as jousting and participating in tournaments. Edward IV overindulged in his appetite for food and conducted extramarital affairs with various mistresses, with whom several illegitimate children were born. Mancini wrote:

> In food and drink he was most immoderate: it was his habit, so I have learned, to take an emetic for the delight of gorging his stomach once more. For this reason and for the case, which was especially dear to him after his recovery of the crown, he had grown fat in the loins, whereas previously he had been not only tall but rather lean and very active. He was licentious in the extreme: more over it was said that he had been most insolent to numerous women after he had seduced them, for, as soon as he grew weary of dalliance,

Edward IV. (Wellcome collection)

he gave up the ladies much against their will to the other courtiers. He pursued with no discrimination the married and unmarried, the noble and the lowly: however, he took none by force. He overcame all by money and promises, and having conquered them, he dismissed them. Although he had many promoters and companions of his vices, the more important and especial were three of the aforementioned relatives of the queen, her two sons and one of her brothers.[94]

Edward was credited for good governance and avoided going to war, which meant that when he died he was the first English king to die solvent since Edward II.

---

94. Ibid., p.93.

68

Eltham Palace

The last visit of Edward IV to Eltham Palace in 1482.

The first record of a manor house at Eltham, south-east London, was in the Domesday survey of 1086, which listed it as belonging to Odo, Bishop of Bayeux, half-brother of William the Conqueror. Edward IV was responsible for the construction of the great hall and the stone bridge that still exist today.

By the fourteenth century, Eltham Palace had evolved into a large, moated royal residence due to renovations carried out during the reign of Richard II. Henry VI lived here as a child, and during 1445 new buildings were constructed in preparation for the arrival of his bride, Margaret of Anjou. They would spend the early part of their marriage at Eltham Palace, and a library was built to accommodate Henry's books. During February 1450 a firebolt struck the palace, causing a fire that caused significant damage to the property. Henry VI stayed at Eltham Castle after the Lancastrian defeat at Northampton in 1460.

Eltham Palace, exterior of the Great Hall. (Author's collection)

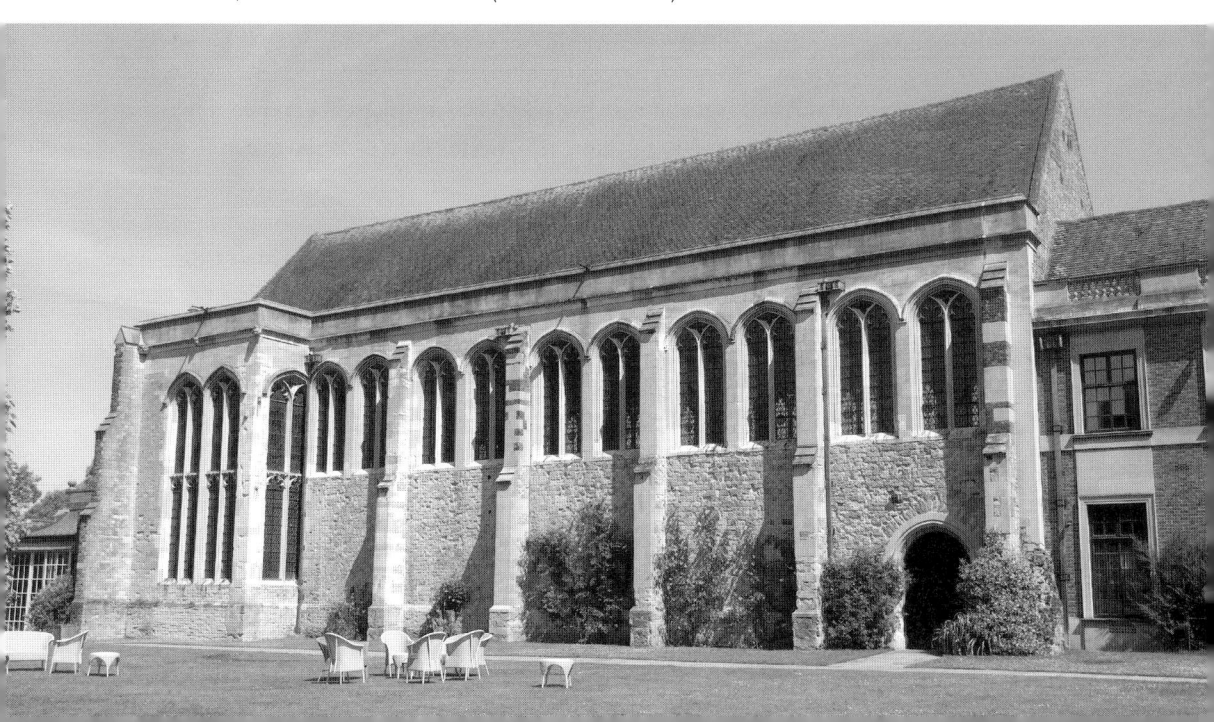

It became the favourite residence of Edward IV and it was here that he spent Christmas with his new bride, Queen Elizabeth, during Christmas 1464. In 1479, Edward brought his family to live at the palace to avoid the plague in London. It was there that two of his ten children were born, Catherine, on 14 August 1479, and Bridget, on 10 November 1480.

On securing a treaty with France that meant the country's wealth did not need to be spent on fighting wars, Edward IV could afford to invest in renovating his palaces. In 1475 Edward IV ordered the expansion of Eltham Palace, including the construction of the great hall, and replaced the timber bridge that crossed the moat with the stone bridge that exists today. The hall has survived six centuries and it was here during Christmas 1482 that Edward held a sumptuous banquet for 2,000 people, including his brother, Richard, Duke of Gloucester. This was Edward's last visit to Eltham because four months later he caught a cold while fishing on the Thames and died at Windsor Castle on 9 April 1483.

Above left: The Great Hall at Eltham Palace. (Author's collection)

Above right: The stone bridge across the moat at Eltham Palace. (Author's collection)

69

St George's Chapel, Windsor Castle

Death of Edward IV.

Edward IV began the redevelopment of St George's Chapel in 1475. He wanted it to become a mausoleum for the House of York. The lodgings and hall of the vicars-choral were demolished to the west of the original chapel to make way for its expansion. He wanted to construct a grand chapel that would become a visual symbol of the new Yorkist dynasty that he was heading and to cement their position as permanent, lawful rulers of the realm. The building is a fine example of Perpendicular architecture, which was commonplace in England during the late Middle Ages and featured large windows, tall towers with battlements and four centred arches. After Edward died on 9 April 1483, he was buried in St George's Chapel. Two of his children who predeceased him were also interred within the chapel: his third son, George, in 1479 and his second daughter, Mary, in 1482.

St George's Chapel is the spiritual home of the Order of St George, which was established in 1348 during the reign of Edward III and consists of the king and twenty-five knights, appointed by the monarch. Each knight was obligated to display a banner of his arms, together with a helmet and sword. Edward IV installed his brothers, George and Richard, together with his brother-in-law, Anthony Woodville, 2nd Earl Rivers, to the order at St George's Chapel. Richard III continued the tradition and invested several knights to the Order of the Garter, including Thomas Stanley and Thomas Howard.

Edward IV had reigned in total for twenty-three years and ruled for twelve years without his position being challenged. Although obese, he was considered to be in good health, but he died after catching a chill at Westminster Palace on 9 April 1483. He was three weeks away from his forty-first birthday. The *Croyland Chronicle* confirmed that he was 'neither worn out with old age nor yet seized with any known kind of malady'.[95]

Laying naked except for a cloth that covered him from the naval to his knees, Edward's body was displayed at Westminster Palace for twelve hours immediately after he died, so that the lords, mayor and aldermen of London could pay their respects and see proof that he was dead.

---

95. Riley, *Croyland*, op. cit., p.483.

St George's Chapel, Windsor. (Courtesy of Aurelien Guichard)

During the following morning his body was transferred to St Stephen's Chapel, Westminster, where it remained for eight days of mourning.

After a funeral ceremony in Westminster Abbey on 17 April, Edward IV was brought to Windsor for burial. A further two days of solemn religious rituals followed and then his remains were interred in St George's Chapel according to his wishes on 19 April 1483. His tomb had been brought from abroad during the previous year and it was so heavy that its weight broke the crane lifting it.[96]

After his ascension, Richard III commissioned a two-storey chantry dedicated to Edward in the north choir aisle, which bears his emblems. Richard also ordered the remains of Henry VI be exhumed from Chertsey Abbey and interred within the chapel, which took place on 12 August 1484. Queen Elizabeth Woodville, who died in 1492, was also buried within St George's Chapel. Although Richard III had ordered the execution of William, 1st Lord Hastings, in 1483, he allowed his body to be interred in a tomb at St George's Chapel close to Edward IV in accordance with Hastings' will.

---

96. Stratford, Laurence, *Edward IV* (Pitman & Sons, London, 1910), p.316.

70

Rose and Crown Inn, Stony Stratford

Richard, Duke of Gloucester, intercepted his nephew, Edward V, at Stony Stratford.

Edward IV passed through Stony Stratford on 30 April 1464 on his journey to besiege castles that were controlled by the Lancastrians. Nineteen years later, his son, Edward V, lodged at the Rose and Crown at Stony Stratford on 29 April 1483 on his journey from Ludlow Castle to London for his coronation. The inn is now a residential house and a plaque confirms that it was here where Richard, Duke of Gloucester (Richard III), seized the uncrowned boy King Edward.

Edward, Prince of Wales, was aged 12 when his father, Edward IV, died. He held court at Ludlow Castle under the guardianship of his uncle, Anthony Woodville, 2nd Earl Rivers, with whom he had developed a close bond.

Gloucester was appointed Protector by Edward IV, but the Woodvilles had refused to acknowledge him in that capacity and decided to discard the king's wishes, and crown Edward V as soon as possible so they could rule England through the boy. Gloucester wanted to execute his brother's wishes and in order to achieve this, he had to take custody of his charge. Gloucester had written to Edward V to confirm the route of his journey from Ludlow Castle to London for the coronation and had arranged to meet his nephew in Northampton to accompany him on the final stage of the journey to the capital in his role as Protector. On 29 April 1483, Gloucester arrived at Northampton with Henry Stafford, 2nd Duke of Buckingham, to learn that the boy king had passed through Northampton and had proceeded to Stony Stratford. Edward sent his uncle, Anthony Woodville, Earl Rivers, to Northampton to explain that they went to Stony Stratford because the retinues of Gloucester and the king could not be accommodated in Northampton. Gloucester invited Rivers to dine and stay with him in Northampton for the night before joining the king in the morning.

The meeting with Rivers was cordial, but when Rivers retired to his bed after dinner, Gloucester was joined by Buckingham, who had held a grudge against the Woodvilles. Both men may have realised that the Woodvilles could obstruct Gloucester in executing the wishes of his brother, Edward IV, and that they must act at Stony Stratford. Gloucester was also fearful that if the Woodvilles exerted too much influence upon Edward V, then his own position could

This building was the former Rose & Crown Inn where, according to the plaque, Richard, Duke of Gloucester, captured his nephew, the uncrowned King Edward V. (Courtesy of Malcolm Campbell; www.geograph.org.uk)

be threatened. They conceived a plan to arrest the Woodvilles and take custody of Edward V with force under the guise of ensuring that he reached London safely for the coronation.

During the following morning, 30 April, before entering Stony Stratford, Gloucester and Buckingham arrested Rivers, together with the king's stepbrother, Lord Richard Grey, and Sir Thomas Vaughan, and sent them to Pomfret Castle, today known as Pontefract, where they were executed on 25 June 1483. Gloucester dismissed the Woodvilles' supporters and proceeded to London with the king, with his own entourage. According to the *Croyland Chronicle*:

> the Duke of Gloucester ... was the ringleader in this outbreak, did not omit or refuse to pay every mark of respect to the king, his nephew in the way of uncovering the head,

bending his knee, or other posture of the body required in a subject. He asserted that the only care was for the protection of his own person, as he knew for certain that there were men in attendance upon the king who had conspired against both his honour and his very existence.[97]

Gloucester's actions at Stony Stratford were regarded as a coup, although he was acting legally and legitimately according to the wishes of Edward IV because the Woodvilles were obstructing him in fulfilling his responsibility as the king's Protector. Gloucester was acting as a loyal servant to the king and in the best interests of the kingdom. The situation was complex because, although Gloucester was acting legally, Edward V would have been concerned for Earl Rivers as he had a close relationship with his uncle, whom he respected and trusted. At the same time, he would have become suspicious of the actions of Gloucester, for although he was also his uncle, he was a stranger to him.

Gloucester was complying with his brother's wishes in accepting the duties of Lord Protector in supporting his nephew. At Stony Stratford, Gloucester may not have intended to seize the throne and maybe was asserting his position to support Edward V as Lord Protector, but at the same time he was isolating the close family members who were trusted by the young king. This was a pivotal moment because Gloucester had instigated a chain of events that he could not reverse, and subsequently Gloucester was placed in a precarious situation where he had a choice of continuing to be loyal and support the king, running the risk of later being cast aside and potentially being destroyed by the Woodvilles, or exceeding his mandate as Lord Protector and pushing forward his own ambition to become king.

---

97. Riley, *Croyland*, op. cit., p.487.

71

Crosby Hall

The London home of Richard III.

During his brief tenure as Lord Protector, prior to seizing the crown, Richard, Duke of Gloucester, established his London headquarters at Crosby Hall, Bishopsgate. The house was built in 1466 using stone and timber for Sir John Crosby, a wool merchant, who served as a sheriff and an alderman in 1470. Crosby was knighted by Edward IV in 1471 and died four years later in 1475. Richard met his council in Crosby Hall while in London. In 1910 Crosby Hall was dismantled and rebuilt at Cheyne Walk, Chelsea, and the great hall is all that remains of the Plantagenet town house.

Despite England living under the shadow of civil unrest, London was regarded as a wealthy, international economic hub. Merchant ships would arrive in London daily from around Flanders and the Mediterranean. Merchants like Sir John Crosby became prosperous and his home is a fine example of his affluence. Edward IV and Richard III depended on merchantmen to borrow money from in return for tax concessions. The interests of London merchants dictated Edward's domestic and foreign policy.

Gloucester and Buckingham arrived in London on 4 May with Edward V and used Crosby Hall as a base where he would convene with his council. At this point Edward V took centre stage as he entered the capital in advance of the coronation. The coronation of the king was meant to have taken place on that day but it was deferred to 24 June. Unable to be with his mother, who had sought sanctuary in Westminster Abbey, Gloucester sent Edward to the Bishop of London's palace next to St Paul's Cathedral. While at Crosby Hall, Gloucester received the Great Seal and passed it to Cardinal Thomas Bourchier, Archbishop of Canterbury. Gloucester wore black in mourning for Edward IV and ordered the mayor and aldermen of the City of London to swear allegiance to Edward V. These actions might suggest that Gloucester was loyal to his nephew at this time.

On 4 May Gloucester announced that the Woodvilles were plotting against him and that they were responsible for the coup that took place in Stony Stratford. Four days later, on 8 May, the council officially made Gloucester Lord Protector on the understanding that the appointment was temporary until Edward V was crowned on 24 June. The council also decreed that Edward V should be transferred to the royal apartments at the Tower of London.

Crosby Hall. (BasPhoto/Shutterstock)

Gloucester remained at Crosby Hall, where he was joined by his wife, Anne Neville, on 5 June 1483. Their son, Edward, was not well enough to travel to London, so he was left to convalesce at Middleham Castle. Gloucester stayed at Crosby Hall until mid-June and then he relocated to Baynard's Castle.

Crosby Hall was dismantled during 1910 and rebuilt at Cheyne Walk on land that was once owned by Sir Thomas More, Richard III's Tudor biographer who helped to perpetuate the notion that he was a villain.

72

Entrance to Westminster Abbey

Birthplace of Edward V and sanctuary for Elizabeth Woodville.

It was at Cheyneygates, within Westminster Abbey, that Queen Elizabeth first sought sanctuary in 1470. Despite being on opposing sides, Henry VI sent food and wine to her during her confinement prior to giving birth to Edward V on 2 November. Thirteen years later, Queen Elizabeth learned that Richard, Duke of Gloucester, had taken Edward V into custody at Stony Gate, and that her brother, Earl Rivers, and son, Sir Richard Grey, had been arrested. Feeling isolated and vulnerable and being unpopular in court, she sought sanctuary with her daughters and her younger son, Richard of Shrewsbury, Duke of York, at Cheyneygates on 30 April 1483.

Archbishop Rotherham of York brought the Chancellor's seal to the Queen at Cheyneygates but by 1 May, the Woodvilles were unable to gather support. The London population had sided with Richard and a messenger was sent to reclaim the seal. Richard's supporters in boats in the River Thames ensured that they were completely isolated. Elizabeth and her family were in a precarious situation, for when Richard and Buckingham arrived in London on 4 May, he announced that the Woodvilles were plotting against them. They would remain in the sanctuary of Cheyneygates for six weeks, until 16 June when Elizabeth permitted her son Richard, Duke of York, to leave the sanctuary of Westminster Abbey to join his brother, Edward V, in the Tower of London prior to the coronation, which was scheduled to take place on 24 June.

According to Mancini, Richard, Duke of Gloucester, realised that the Duke of York was the next in line of succession and would impede his own ambitions to reign as king. Gloucester arranged the date of the coronation and suggested to the council that it was imperative that Edward should be crowned in the presence of his brother. Gloucester also added that the Duke of York was being held within Cheyneygates against his will by his mother and that he should be liberated. Supported by the council, Gloucester surrounded Cheyneygates with troops. On 16 June, Elizabeth surrendered her son to Cardinal Thomas Bourchier, Archbishop of Canterbury, who despite pledging his faith to Edward IV, took the young Duke of York to Gloucester at the Tower of London. On the same day Gloucester rescheduled the coronation of Edward V to 9 November.

Entrance into Westminster Abbey. Queen Elizabeth would seek sanctuary in the part of Westminster Abbey known as Cheyneygates. (Kevin George/Shutterstock)

Elizabeth Woodville and her daughters remained in the sanctuary of Cheyneygates until 1 March 1484 after Richard III took a public oath to support them and find suitable marriages for his nieces. Elizabeth's son, Sir Richard Grey, and her brother, Anthony Woodville, 2nd Earl Rivers, had been executed at Pontefract Castle during the previous year. It must be considered that during this period, the little princes, Edward V and Richard, Duke of York, had not been seen since the previous summer and some historians believe that Elizabeth may not have thought that Richard III was responsible for their fate and rumoured death. If she did harbour fears that he had murdered them, she may have made the decision to agree to Richard's terms, because he might be on the throne for a long time and she needed to make the best of a bad situation for the future of her remaining children and for her own self-preservation.

73

St Paul's Cross, London

Richard III publicly declares his claim to the throne.

The statue of St Paul, located in the grounds of St Paul's Cathedral, was erected in 1910 and stands near to the original preaching cross and open-air pulpit named St Paul's Cross.

On 22 June 1483, Dr Ralph Shaa (or Shaw), brother of Edmund Shaa, the Mayor of London, championed Richard, Duke of Gloucester's, legitimacy for the throne at St Paul's Cross. Both Gloucester and Buckingham were present at St Paul's Cross when Dr Ralph Shaa questioned the validity of Edward IV's marriage to Elizabeth Woodville, claiming that he was already contractually obligated to marry Eleanor Butler, who later married and became Lady Eleanor Talbot. This fact could not be substantiated because Eleanor died in 1468, but during 1476–77, Elizabeth Woodville had raised concerns as to whether her husband had been married to Eleanor. At that time Robert Stillington, Bishop of Bath and Wells, had intimated to George, Duke of Clarence, that he had conducted this marriage ceremony, when Clarence was plotting against Edward IV.

Shaa further questioned the legitimacy of the sons of Edward IV, asserting that they were conceived in adultery and did not resemble their grandfather, Richard, Duke of York, who was killed at Wakefield. Support for the line of succession to bypass the sons of Edward IV and pass to Richard, Duke of Gloucester, was proclaimed at these sermons. Challenging the validity of the marriage between Edward IV and Elizabeth Woodville and the legitimacy of their children would form the justification for Richard's claim to the throne and the basis for the document entitled *Titulus Regius* (the Royal Title) that would be presented to Parliament that discredited the reign of Edward IV, declared his marriage to Elizabeth Woodville was invalid and that their children, Edward V, Richard, Duke of York, and Elizabeth were illegitimate, annulling their claim to the throne. It also claimed that Elizabeth Woodville had seduced Edward IV through witchcraft.

The parentage of Edward IV was also questioned during the sermon, alleging that his mother, Cecily, had conceived him with another man, a claim without substantiation other than that that his features and physique did not resemble that of Richard, Duke of York. At the risk of damaging and disrespecting the reputation of his mother Cecily, Richard, Duke of Gloucester, was prepared to slander his own family to further his argument to claim the throne. There is no record of how the slander of Cecily's reputation, questioning the parentage of his brother, Edward IV, had affected Richard's relationship with his mother.

On 24 June, Buckingham presented the argument to Parliament against placing a boy on the throne and reminded them of the problems that had arisen during the minority of Henry VI. Parliament agreed and ratified the *Titulus Regius*, which proclaimed Gloucester as King Richard III and it was confirmed six months later during the only session of Parliament during January 1484. A combination of ambition, the stability of the nation and a deep resentment for the Woodville family may have been the primary motivations and justification in Richard taking matters into his own hands and usurping his nephew's throne.

The statue of St Paul stands close to where St Paul's Cross stood during the Wars of the Roses. (Author's collection)

74

Baynard's Castle, London

Richard, Duke of Gloucester, requested to take the English throne at Baynard's Castle.

A castle had existed on the northern bank of the Thames that extended to Upper Thames Street, between where Blackfriars Bridge and the Millennium Bridge now stands, since Ralph Baynard, a Norman knight, built a fortification around 1086. Named Baynard's Castle, it was demolished by King John in 1213. A second castle bearing the same name was rebuilt by Humphrey, Duke of Gloucester, south-east of the original castle in 1428. Ownership of the castle reverted to the Crown when Gloucester died in 1447 and Henry VI granted it to Richard, Duke of York.

Baynard's Castle became the London headquarters of the House of York during the Wars of the Roses. Richard, Duke of York, came to Baynard's Castle on 10 October 1460 after his brief sojourn in Ireland to be reunited with his wife, Cecily. He would spend the last days with his family there before his death at Wakefield. Cecily would reside at her London residence of Baynard's Castle during widowhood until her death in 1495.

It was here at Baynard's Castle where Edward IV was proclaimed king during 1461, and he stayed here frequently while in London. He was reunited with Elizabeth and his children when he returned from exile in 1471. During the middle of June 1483, Richard, Duke of Gloucester, vacated Crosby Hall and lived at Baynard's Castle, where on 26 June, he received a bill of petition from supportive nobles from the Houses of Lords and Commons, including Henry Stafford, 2nd Duke of Buckingham, and Thomas Stanley. They championed him as the rightful heir and offered him the crown of England. The following day he accepted the crown in the audience chamber.

Henry VII expanded Baynard's Castle during his reign, adding a tall octagonal tower in the centre of the palace and three additional wings. His wife, Elizabeth of York, frequently resided at the castle and it was here where she stayed with Henry VII and Arthur on the evening of Arthur's wedding to Catherine of Aragon in 1501.

Baynard's Castle was destroyed in 1666 during the Great Fire of London. The only indication that Baynard's Castle once stood on the site where the City of London School is now located is a blue plaque.

Plaque commemorating the site of Baynard's Castle, London. (Author's collection)

Baynard's Castle on the north bank of the River Thames. (Wellcome Collection)

75

The Coronation Chair

Richard III crowned at his coronation in Westminster Abbey on 6 July 1483.

The Coronation Chair was made under the orders of King Edward I to enclose the Stone of Scone, which had been taken from Scotland and transferred to Westminster Abbey in 1296. It was built of oak and completed in 1301. This throne was used during the coronation of thirty-eight English monarchs, including the four kings, Henry VI, Edward IV, Richard III and Henry VII, who reigned during the Wars of the Roses. Edward V never got the chance to sit on this chair to be crowned King of England.

After executing several prominent supporters of Edward IV, Richard proclaimed that his nephews, Edward V and Richard, were illegitimate and asserted himself as rightful heir to the throne. The coronation of Richard III was prepared swiftly and he ordered that 6,000 troops he had summoned from his estates in the north and those belonging to Henry Stafford, 2nd Duke of Buckingham, loyal to his cause, remain in the City of London to maintain order in the event of civil dissent. He also imposed a curfew for three nights after 10.00 pm and prohibited the bearing of arms.

The coronation took place at Westminster Abbey on 6 July 1483. Richard and his wife, Anne, proceeded from Whitehall Palace to Westminster Hall, where they walked barefoot upon cloth to Westminster Abbey. Richard wore a purple velvet gown. The king's procession comprised Cardinal Thomas Bourchier, Archbishop of Canterbury; followed by Northumberland carrying the Sword of Mercy; Thomas, Baron Stanley, bearing the Lord High Constable's Mace; and John de la Pole, 2nd Duke of Suffolk (brother-in-law of Richard III) carrying the sceptre. John Howard, 1st Duke of Norfolk, carried the crown, while his son, Thomas Howard, Earl of Surrey, brought the Sword of State. Richard III's train was carried by Buckingham. The queen's procession followed the king into Westminster Abbey and Anne's train was carried by Lady Margaret Beaufort, the mother of Henry Tudor, who later became Henry VII, and grandmother of Henry VIII.

The coronation service was conducted by Cardinal Bourchier. The ceremony was grand and attended by most of the peers in England. At the altar, Richard and Anne were anointed with the sacramental oil. Once they had changed their clothes to cloth of gold, they were crowned

The Coronation Chair, Westminster Abbey, on which Henry VI, Edward IV and Richard III were crowned. (Copyright Dean and Chapter of Westminster)

by the cardinal. He had crowned three kings during his tenure, including Edward IV and Henry VII. According to Mancini, 'the cardinal of Canterbury, albeit reluctantly, anointed and crowned the King of England'.[98] Anne was crowned alongside Richard – the daughter of the kingmaker, Richard Neville, 16th Earl of Warwick, was now Queen of England. This was the first joint coronation since the accession of Edward II and Isabella of France 175 years earlier. In a break from tradition, Richard III swore the oath in English and insisted that the holy oil should be kept with the other regalia for the future. After the crowning, *Te Deum* was sung and Richard and Anne received communion before adjourning to Westminster Hall for the coronation banquet. Within two years of her coronation, Anne was buried in Westminster Abbey after her death on 16 March 1485.

---

98. Carson, Annette, *Domenico Mancini de occupatione regni Anglie* (Imprimis Imprimatur, Horstead, 2021), p.71.

76

Westminster Hall

Coronation banquet of Richard III.

Westminster Hall was built between 1097 and 1099 during the reign of William II (Rufus) and has played a prominent role in the history of England and the United Kingdom. During the nine centuries of its existence, it has been used as a place for political debate, trials of traitors of the state, royal banquets, feasts and ceremonies. The resplendent hammer beam roof was commissioned by Richard II in 1393 and built by Henry Yevele, the king's chief mason, and the carpenter, Henry Herland.

Westminster Hall is connected with various prominent events that took place during the Wars of the Roses. On 4 March 1461, Edward IV sat in regal splendour at the high dais, where he received the royal sceptre.

On 9 May 1483, after Cardinal Bourchier persuaded Queen Elizabeth that her son, Richard, Duke of York, should join his brother Edward V in the Tower of London, the young prince was taken to the hall. He was passed to Buckingham, who then led him to the Star Chamber and he was handed over into the custody of Richard, Duke of Gloucester.

Richard, Duke of Gloucester, took his seat on the marble chair of the King's Bench in Westminster Hall on 26 June 1483, where he effectually usurped his nephew, Edward V, and was proclaimed Richard III, King of England. He was supported by Lord Howard and his brother-in-law, the Duke of Suffolk. According to the *Croyland Chronicle*:

> it was set forth, by way of prayer, in an address in a certain roll of parchment, that the sons of king Edward were bastards, on the ground that he had contracted a marriage with one lady Eleanor Botelar before his marriage to queen Elizabeth; added to which, the blood of his older brother, George, Duke of Clarence, had been attained; so that, at the present time, no certain and uncorrupted lineal blood could be found of Richard, Duke of York, except in the person of the said Richard, Duke of Gloucester. For which reason, he was entreated, at the end of the said roll on part of the lords and commons of the realm, to assume his lawful rights.[99]

---

99. Riley, *Croyland*, op. cit., p.489.

Westminster Hall. (Gimas/Shutterstock)

Irrespective of the confusion caused by the legal complexities that supported Richard's claim to the throne, it was publicly accepted. Two weeks later, on 6 July, when he returned to Westminster Hall as king for the banquet celebrating his coronation. John Howard, 1st Duke of Norfolk, rode into the hall on his charger to disperse the spectators so that the celebrations could begin. The king and queen entered the hall at 4.00 pm and sat on a table on the dais overlooking the hall, where there were four large tables that accommodated their guests including bishops, barons and noblemen accompanied by their ladies. They were offered a feast of forty-six different dishes that included mutton, beef and peacock. Stretched prone at Richard's feet were two knights and he and his wife were served by his childhood friends, Viscount Lovell and Sir Robert Percy, together with Surrey, Norfolk and Lord Audley (who served as carver). Sir Robert Dymock, the king's champion, entered Westminster Hall on a steed, dressed in armour at the beginning of the second course to present the challenge. Dymock drank to the health of the king and retired with the cup as his reward. Clarions and trumpets concluded the banquet after the third course.

77

Arms of Richard III, Charter of Incorporation Plaque, Gloucester

Richard III visited Gloucester during his royal progress in 1483.

The Coat of Arms of Richard III and a plaque were presented to Gloucester by the Richard III Society in 1983 to commemorate the five-hundredth anniversary of him presenting the Charter of Incorporation to the city. They are displayed on the wall of St Michael's Tower in Eastgate Street, The second and third quarters show three English lions, while the first and fourth display the French fleur-de-lys, with a white lion and a white boar.

Richard III was made duke of the city when he was aged 8 in 1461. Ten years later, in 1471, the city became pivotal as Queen Margaret and her soldiers tried to use its bridges to cross the River Severn into Wales to join Jasper Tudor. Edward IV and Richard, as Duke of Gloucester, dashed from Windsor with the Yorkist army to prevent this happening, but the Lancastrian army reached the town first and demanded entry. The people of the city remained loyal to Richard when he was Duke of Gloucester and refused to open the gates, forcing Margaret to proceed to the nearest crossing at Tewkesbury.

Soon after his coronation, Richard was keen to assert himself as sovereign by embarking on a royal progress to the north of England so that he could be seen as the legitimate ruler. The route passed through the City of London, Windsor, Oxford, Tewkesbury, Gloucester, Worcester and Coventry before culminating in York. Richard arrived in Gloucester towards the end of July 1483.

Richard III was popular in Gloucester and, remembering its refusal to allow Queen Margaret to enter its walls three months earlier before the Battle of Tewkesbury, he granted it special concessions with a charter in which he stated 'because of the special affection which we bear towards the said town of Gloucester'.[100] It was usual tradition for towns to pay a large fee for their charters, but one of the benefits that Richard bestowed upon Gloucester for 'good and faithful actions … in causes of particular importance to us,'[101] was that the town only had to

---

100. www.gloucestershire.gov.uk/archives.

101. Ibid.

Coat of Arms of Richard III and a plaque, Gloucester. (Courtesy of Phillip Halling; www.geograph.org.uk)

pay a third of its annual tax to the Exchequer. Other privileges permitted by the charter was the appointment of a sheriff, elected mayor and aldermen, as well as the appointment of a coroner. Richard was also responsible for creating the county of Gloucestershire, comprising thirty villages and with the associated taxes owed.

78

York Minster

Richard III's first visit to York as monarch.

A church was built on this site after the Norman conquest, but was burnt down in 1187. Construction of York Minster began during the thirteenth century and the central and western towers were built during the middle of the fourteenth century. It took 200 years to construct the existing Gothic church. The Cathedral and Metropolitan Church of St Peter, known as York Minster, has strong connections with Richard III.

After the death of Edward IV on 9 April 1483, Richard, Duke of Gloucester, was proclaimed Lord Protector of his successor and attended a commemorative service at York Minster. It was also an opportunity for Richard to lead the nobility in making an oath of allegiance to his nephew, Edward V. This happened before he felt that his own position as protector was under threat.

Aerial photo of York Minster. (Neil Mitchell/Shutterstock)

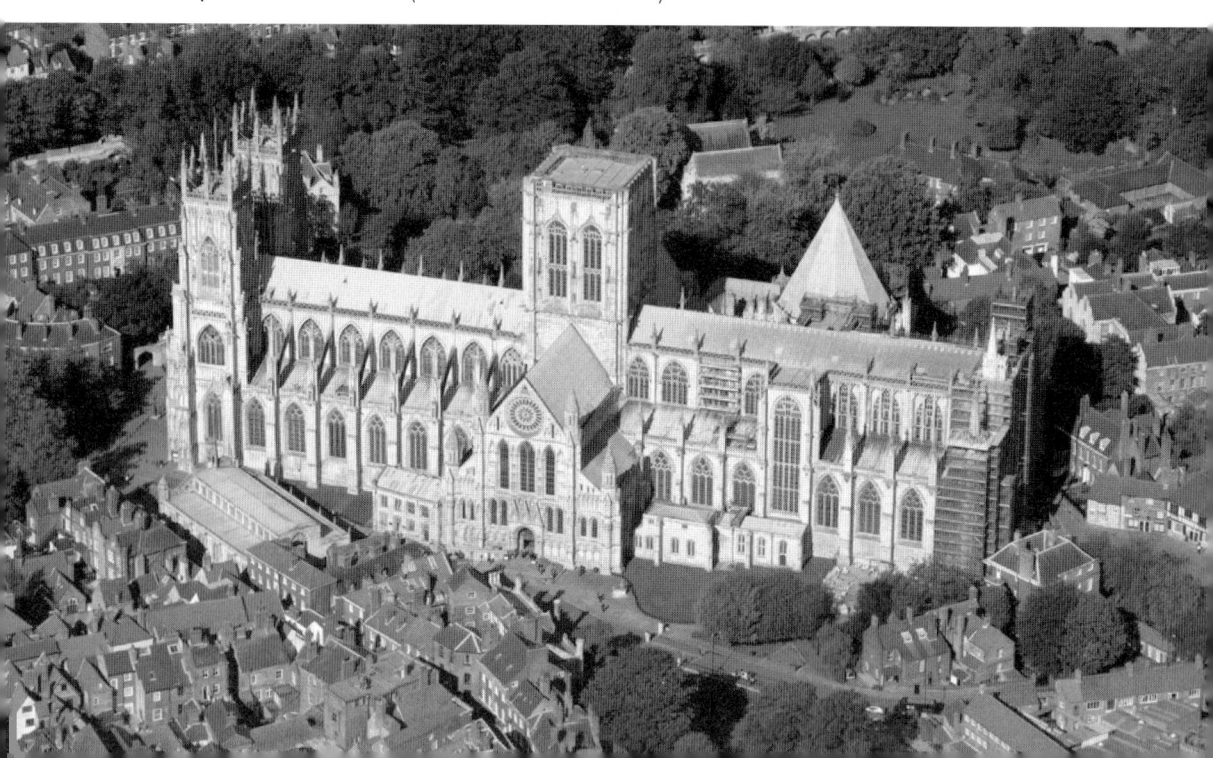

The West Door at York Minster where Richard III was received in 1483. (Author's collection)

Five months after proclaiming his allegiance to Edward V, Richard returned to York as king when, on 29 August 1483, his procession passed through the streets of the city. He was accompanied by his wife, Queen Anne, and his son alongside an entourage of prominent clergymen and nobles. They were received by the dean and canon at the west door of York Minster, where he was sprinkled with holy water, before a service was dedicated in his honour. This ceremony marked the beginning of a three-week stay in the city.

Richard and Anne returned to York Minster on 8 September 1483 to attend mass conducted by the Bishop of Durham before the investiture of Edward as Prince of Wales, which took place in the adjacent archbishop's palace that day. Richard and Anne wore their crowns, which prompted speculation that a second coronation had taken place within York Minster.

During his reign Richard had planned to provide financial support for a chantry at York Minster to accommodate 100 priests who would pray for him and the royal family, but this initiative was curtailed by his death at Bosworth.

79

Archbishop's Palace, York

The investiture of Edward of Middleham, Prince of Wales, was held here.

The Archbishop's Palace was the official residence of the Archbishop of York during the Middle Ages. The chapel of the Archbishop's Palace where Edward was invested as Prince of Wales is now used as the Minster Library and is located in Dean's Park, just north of York Minster.

Another reason for the visit to York was for the investiture of Edward as Prince of Wales, aged 10, which took place in the Archbishop's Palace, adjacent to York Minister. The investiture that took place on 8 September 1483, and involved Edward being knighted, a garland wreath being placed upon his head and a golden ring placed on his finger. According to the *Croyland Chronicle* 'here, on a day appointed for repeating his coronation in the metropolitan church, he also presented his only son, Edward, whom, on the same day he had elevated to the rank of Prince of Wales, with the insignia of the golden wand, and the wreath upon the head; while, at the same time, he gave most gorgeous and sumptuous feasts and banquets, for the purpose of gaining the affections of the people'.[102]

Polydore Vergil also wrote of the positive reception that Richard received from the people of York, possibly taken from personal testimonies:

> There was a great confluence of people for desire of beholding the new king. In which procession, very solemnly set forth and celebrated by the clergy, the king was present in person, adorned with a notably rich diadem, and accompanied with a great number of noble men, the queen followed, also with crown upon her head, who led by her hand her son Edward, crowned also with so great honour, joy and congratulation of the inhabitants, as in show of rejoicing they extolled King Richard above the skies.[103]

---

102. Riley, *Croyland*, op. cit., p.490.

103. Vergil, Polydore, *English History Comprising the Reigns of Henry VI, Edward IV and Richard III* (J.B. Nichols & Sons, London, 1844), p.190.

Chapel of the Archbishop's Palace in York, where Edward of Middleham was invested as Prince of Wales. Photo taken from the York Minster Tower. (Author's collection)

Edward's half-brother, John of Gloucester, fathered by Richard III, who was born in 1468, was also knighted during that day. After the ceremonies, a feast to celebrate the occasion took place in the Archbishop's Palace and this lasted for four hours during that evening.

Above: Chapel of the Archbishop's Palace in York, where Edward of Middleham was invested as Prince of Wales. (Author's collection)

Below: Plaque commemorating the investiture of Edward as Prince of Wales. (Author's collection)

80

The Bloody Tower, Tower of London

Edward V and Richard, Duke of York, incarcerated in the Bloody Tower.

Constructed in 1220, the Bloody Tower was originally called the Garden Tower because the west window overlooked the Lieutenant's Garden. The lower part of the tower formed part of the main river entrance into the castle. In 1270, the Outer Ward was built, which moved the River Thames away and this tower became a land entrance. It became known as the Bloody Tower during the mid-sixteenth century due to its notorious association with the two princes.

Edward V, aged 12, and his brother Richard of Shrewsbury, Duke of York, aged 9, were accommodated within the Garden Tower from May 1483. Edward V arrived at the Tower of London between 9 and 19 May 1483. At that time, the Tower of London's sinister reputation as a state prison had not been cemented, which happened during the Tudor period. The fortress had been used as a royal residence since its construction during the eleventh century, being used by future monarchs prior to coronation or as a refuge in times of civil disorder. So, the

Southern façade of the Bloody Tower. (Courtesy of Ethan Doyle White; via Wikimedia Commons)

Interior of the Bloody Tower as it would have looked when Sir Walter Raleigh was imprisoned within these walls a century after the two princes occupied this space. (Author's collection)

two princes had been brought here by their uncle, Richard, Duke of Gloucester, for their own protection and at first there seemed nothing to fear. They were living in comfortable surroundings within the building that is now known as the Bloody Tower. It was tradition for the successive monarch to be brought to the Tower of London before the coronation. The two princes were reported to have been last seen on 16 June 1483 shooting arrows in the garden and it is believed that they were then transferred to the White Tower, probably after they were declared illegitimate on 22 June at St Paul's Cross.

During July 1483, fifty men tried to incite an uprising to free the two princes from the Tower of London. They set fires in the capital to cause a diversion as they tried to access the Tower, but the plot failed and four of the conspirators were executed. This highlighted the problem to Richard III that so long as the two boys were alive, his crown would not be secure.

81

Staircase where two skeletons were discovered

Possible remains of the two princes.

During renovation work beneath a staircase within the White Tower during 1674, the skeletons of two children were discovered.

It is believed that the two princes were transferred to the White Tower during the summer of 1483, while Richard III was conducting a royal progress of the northern counties. It is believed that they were then murdered by an unknown assailant, because they disappeared without trace. Their servants had been dismissed on 18 July. According to Dominic Mancini:

> After the removal of Hastings, all the attendants who had served the young king were barred from access to him. He and his brother were conducted back into the more inward apartments of the Tower itself, and day by day came to be observed more rarely through the lattices and windows, up to the point that they completely ceased to be visible. The physician Argentine, who was the last of the attendants employed by the young king, reported that, like a victim prepared for sacrifice, he sought remission of sins by daily confession and penitence, because he reckoned that his death was imminent … I have seen several men break out in tears and lamentation when mention was made of him after he was removed from men's sight, and now there was suspicion that he had been taken by death.[104]

People in London were already saying to Dominic Mancini just before he left the country at the end of July 1483 that the princes were probably dead, but the fact could not be substantiated. The *Croyland Chronicle* speculated that 'a rumour was spread that the sons of King Edward had died a violent death, but it was uncertain how'.[105]

Tudor chroniclers attributed the blame for their deaths to Richard III, because he realised that his reign would not be secured so long as his two nephews remained alive. According

---

104. Carson, op. cit., p.65.

105. Riley, *Croyland*, op. cit., p.491.

to Sir Thomas More, Richard was in Warwick when he sent Sir James Tyrell with orders for Robert Brackenbury, Constable of the Tower of London, to deal with the two princes but he refused to execute it. Richard was in Warwick from 7 to 15 August 1483, so it is probable that Brackenbury received the order towards the end of that month. Tyrell is reputed to have smothered the two princes in their beds as they slept. We must note that More was aged 5 when the princes disappeared and that when he wrote his *History of Richard III* between 1512 to 1519, he was more likely to portray a negative, incriminating vision of the Yorkist king. This would later influence William Shakespeare in his play and perpetuate the notion that he was a villain. There may be some truth in More's account, but as modern readers it is possible to consider that More was demonstrating his allegiance to Henry VIII and could have been distorting the truth to disseminate Tudor propaganda in order to preserve the dynasty. It is possible that Richard III was innocent and that he would not have gained anything by the deaths of his nephews under his sanction. If Richard was confident in his own conviction and confidence that his claim to the throne was unquestionable, then he may have thought that there was no need to kill them, but to keep them imprisoned. The disappearance has caused contentious debate between those who believe the Tudor propaganda that said he was responsible and supporters of Richard III who champion his innocence.

The skeletons were found beneath the staircase in the White Tower. (Author's collection)

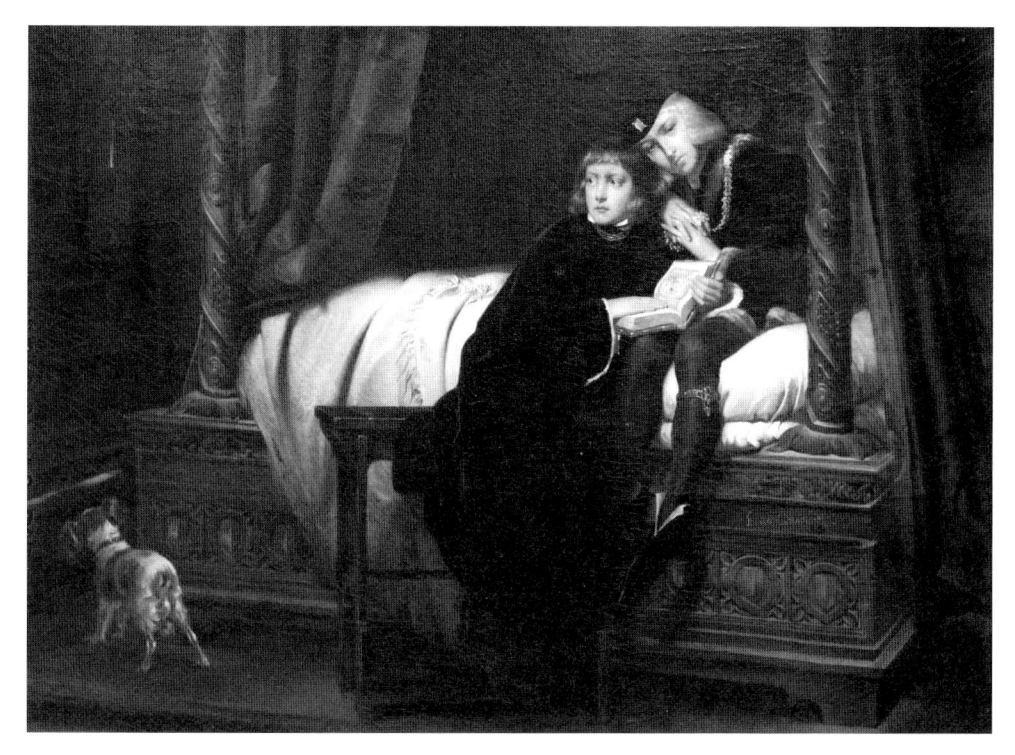

Edward V and Richard, Duke of York, in the Tower of London, depicted by French artist Paul Delaroche. (Louvre Museum Public Domain)

Brackenbury would later be conferred with estates and a knighthood for special services to the Crown and he would die defending Richard III on the battlefield at Bosworth. Sir James Tyrell would later serve Henry VII, but was charged with treason in 1502 on another matter. During his examination, according to More, Tyrell confessed to the murder of the two princes and implicated John Dighton, who corroborated Tyrell's account.

On ascending the stairs to enter the White Tower, on the right there is another staircase where the skeletons of two boys were found on 17 July 1674. This hidden staircase, which leads to the chapel, was revealed when the building protecting the entrance was demolished. It was believed by Charles II that the remains of the little princes had been found and they were reinterred in Westminster Abbey inside a marble urn designed by Sir Christopher Wren close to the tomb of Elizabeth I in the Lady's Chapel. The location of the bones of these skeletons corresponds with Sir Thomas More's book in which he wrote that they were smothered 'and buried at the stair foot meetly deep in the ground under a great heap of stones'.[106] The urn was opened in July 1933 and it was confirmed that the remains belonged to two young children of similar ages to the two princes, although their genders were not ascertained. Given that the remains were never authenticated or identified, the fate of the two princes remains a mystery that will probably never be solved.

---

106. More, Sir Thomas, *The History of King Richard III* (Cambridge University Press, 1883), p.84.

82

Facial Reconstruction of Richard III

This model of Richard III was commissioned by the Richard III Society in 2013. It was constructed by Professor Caroline Wilkinson and the forensic art team at the University of Dundee using data obtained from scans conducted of the skull of Richard III at Leicester Royal Infirmary.

Portraits were altered to show Richard with sharper features and his scoliosis was acerbated into a hunchback as part of the Tudor propaganda machine to discredit his appearance and character. Certainly, Richard was no saint; he was a man of his time where the moral compasses of members of both the houses of Lancaster and York were extremely compromised. The facial reconstruction of Richard III drawn from his skull does not resemble the appearance of a monster or tyrant as depicted by William Shakespeare and Polydore Vergil or contemporary portraits. Vergil perpetuated Tudor propaganda in presenting Richard negatively. Vergil wrote that Richard 'was little of stature, deformed of body, thine shoulder being higher than the other, a short and sour continence, which seemed to savour of mischief, and utter evidently craft and deceit. While he was thinking of any matter, he did continually bite his nether lip, as though that cruel nature of his did so rage against itself in that little carcass.'[107]

During his short reign, which lasted just twenty-six months, Richard III attained several political achievements passed through thirty-three acts of legislation during his only meeting of parliament, which he opened on 23 January 1484. The legislation included the introduction of a fairer judicial system. He championed justice for everyone in society, refining existing legations that would help to create the laws of England. Bribery, intimidation and corruption flourished throughout the justice system, but during his reign Richard ordered that all judges must be impartial and judge cases fairly. Under his tenure the jury system was established and the premise that a person was innocent until proven guilty. He also improved the rights of the accused; bail was introduced to limit imprisonment before a trial and their property and assets could not be seized until conviction. Laws were also passed to protect land ownership and trade. In an attempt to prevent fraud and protect consumer rights, Richard introduced new standards for weights and measures, and required that property rights be recorded. He instituted strict

---

107. Vergil, op. cit., p.226.

The reconstructed head of Richard III. (Nick Atkins/Shutterstock)

import regulations to support English trade against foreign competition. He gained popularity by abolishing the tradition of royal benevolences, which were mandatory payments to the Crown, which his brother Edward IV relied heavily upon to increase the Treasury coffers. Instead of increasing taxes, he ordered tax clerks to scrutinise old documents to search for unpaid dues that needed to be collected. He also removed incompetent and corrupt officials in government, replacing them with able men. Richard encouraged the writing, printing and importation of books and exempted books from taxation. Richard insisted that the laws of the kingdom be written in English instead of French and Latin so that people could understand them, and they were printed for the first time. He believed in the code of medieval chivalry and founded the College of Arms in 1484.

In contrast to his debauched brother, Edward IV, Richard was a pious man, who was intent on restoring morals to the kingdom. He possessed a Book of Hours that contained his own annotations, which suggests that he practised religion and devoted time to daily prayer. However, rumours circulated that he wanted to marry his niece, Elizabeth Woodville, and when his wife, Anne Neville, died, he swore an oath denying that intention.

83

Middleham Castle

Favourite residence of Richard III.

Richard III spent a significant part of his childhood at Middleham Castle in Yorkshire and frequently lived there after he married Anne Neville.

Castles were built for defence and to endure siege warfare, not for domestic comfort. The keep, with 12ft-thick walls, was constructed by Robert Fitzralf during the 1170s on the southern slope of Wensleydale. The castle was acquired by the Neville family during the thirteenth century. It became a favourite residence of Richard Neville, 16th Earl of Warwick, his wife, Anne, and two daughters Isabel and Anne. It was here that Richard, Duke of Gloucester, resided as a child under his guardianship at Middleham Castle from 1462 to 1464. There was no expectation that Richard would one day become king because he was low down in the line of succession. However, while living at Middleham Castle, Warwick's 'Master of Henxman' became a mentor to Richard in becoming a knight, teaching him the skills of horsemanship, combat and jousting. Despite being an unhealthy child, Richard overcame his ailments to enjoy the pursuit of hunting, practising swordsmanship and the use of the lance on the tiltyard. It was here at Middleham Castle that Richard trained for war and to serve his brother, Edward IV, from an early age. He was taught these skills alongside two other boys, Sir Robert Percy and Francis, later Viscount Lovell, and they were to become close friends. Richard would have also known Warwick's daughter, Anne Neville, who was four years his junior.

After his capture at the Battle of Hexham, Lancastrian knight Sir Philip Wentworth was brought to Middleham Castle to be executed on 18 May 1464. Wentworth had served Henry VI loyally during the Wars of the Roses and he was the great-grandfather of Jane Seymour, third wife of Henry VIII, and the great-great-grandfather of Edward VI.

Middleham Castle was granted to Richard in 1471 and this was his primary residence, where he governed while he held the position of Lieutenant of the North as deputy of Edward IV. As Steward of the Duchy of Lancaster, Richard's official residence was at Pontefract Castle but he preferred to stay at Middleham, where he lived for most of Edward IV's reign. It was where he lived with Anne until he ascended the throne. Anne gave birth to their only child, Edward, in the south-eastern tower, which is known as the 'Prince's Tower', circa 1473-76. While Richard and Anne were in Nottingham, Edward died at Middleham Castle on 9 April 1484. His death was a personal tragedy that would undermine Richard's position as king because he no longer had a legitimate successor, although he did have two illegitimate children, named John and Katherine, who were born many years prior to his marriage to Anne.

Above: Middleham Castle, North Yorkshire. (Tim Lamper/Shutterstock)

Right: Statue of Richard III at Middleham Castle. (Courtesy of Leestuartsherriff; via Wikimedia Commons)

84

Nottingham Castle

Richard III raised his standard and marched to Leicester.

William the Conqueror ordered the construction of Nottingham Castle in 1068 and has strong connections with the Wars of the Roses. After the Battle of Mortimer's Cross, Edward, Earl of March, proclaimed himself Edward IV, King of England, from Nottingham Castle in 1461. During the years 1476 to 1480, Edward invested in building the state apartments in the Middle Bailey and strengthening the defences.

Richard III first visited Nottingham Castle during August 1483 on his journey from London to York. He completed the renovation work on the castle that his brother had begun, including a four-storey, six-sided tower that contained a spiral staircase now known as Richard's Tower. This tower was used to provide private accommodation for the king. Richard was known to reside in the tower when he stayed at the castle and hence that is how it got its name. All that remains of Richard's Tower is the base.

It was at Nottingham Castle that Richard III learnt of the death of his son, Edward, at Middleham in April 1484. The *Croyland Chronicle* confirmed that:

> this only son of his, in whom all the hopes of the royal succession, fortified with so many oaths, were centred, was seized with an illness of but short duration, and died at Middleham Castle … being the first of the reign of the said king Richard. On hearing the news of this at Nottingham, where they were then residing, you might have seen his father and mother in a state almost bordering on madness, by reason of their sudden grief.[108]

The bereavement is suspected to have exacerbated the ill health of Queen Anne, who was aged 28, and she died within a year of her son's death from tuberculosis at the Palace of Westminster on 16 March 1485.

Richard III regarded Nottingham Castle as the 'castle of care' and the widowed king returned to establish his headquarters there to devote time to issues relating to the Midlands and to

---

108. Riley, *Croyland*, op. cit., p.497.

The gatehouse was built around 1255 and was used by Richard III and Edward IV to enter the castle. (Valdis Skudre/Shutterstock)

hunt during the summer 1485. When he arrived on 9 June 1485, he was not expecting to suppress a rebellion.

On 16 August, Richard and some close friends went into Sherwood Forest, to Beskwood Lodge (also known as Bestwood Lodge), 6 miles north of Nottingham, where he received news that Henry Tudor had landed in Wales on 7 August. Initially he thought that the landing of the rebels would be contained in Wales and did not feel threatened, so he continued hunting. On the following day he rode to Nottingham Castle, where he sent orders to Brackenbury, Lovell, Norfolk and Northumberland to assemble their men in Leicester. On 19 August, Richard raised his standard at Nottingham Castle and began his journey to Leicester and the battlefield at Bosworth. George Stanley, 7th Baron Strange, was brought under guard as a hostage to ensure that his father, Lord Stanley, remained loyal to Richard and the Yorkist cause. Lord Stanley was not intimidated by Richard's action, joined forces with Henry Tudor and George was released after the Battle of Bosworth.

85

Mill Bay Memorial

Henry Tudor lands near Milford Haven, South Wales

Henry Tudor, 2nd Earl of Richmond, had spent a significant part of his life living in Brittany in exile. When Richard, Duke of Gloucester, disinherited his nephew, Edward V, and seized the throne of England, plans were formulated to replace Richard with Henry Tudor. Proclamations were issued by Richard III on 7 December 1484 and 23 June 1485 denouncing Henry's claim to the throne, based on his mother's lineage through the House of Lancaster being illegitimate and that this line, although legitimated towards the end of the fourteenth century, was forbidden from ascending the throne.

Although Henry Tudor had a weak claim to the English throne, he was one of the few survivors who were related to Henry VI and many opponents of Richard III were rallying behind him. While in France, Henry did not have an army so the King of France supplied him with ships and French mercenaries so he could invade England. On 1 August 1485, Henry Tudor left the French port of Harfleur with an armada comprising fifty-five ships and an army of 4,000 soldiers. Approximately 2,000 of that number were French mercenaries, including some men who were recruited from French jails that were promised liberty in return for serving Henry Tudor.[109]

Among the commanders who accompanied Henry were his uncle, Jasper Tudor, Earl of Pembroke, and John de Vere, 13th Earl of Oxford. After a seven-day passage across the English Channel and Irish Sea towards Wales, Henry Tudor landed at Mill Bay, Milford Haven, on 7 August 1485. This rugged stretch of coastline was a suitable place for the rebels to land because of its remoteness and its sandy beach. Also, the inlet at Mill Bay afforded suitable anchorage for the rebel's flotilla and shelter from rough seas, and it was concealed from Dale Castle, which was positioned inland. Richard's forces were far away and if Henry could establish a foothold in Wales, where he was guaranteed strong support, he could increase the size of his army without interference. This was the first time that Henry had seen the Welsh coastline in fourteen years. On disembarking on the beach, Henry knelt upon his knees and recited the Psalm *me Deus et decerne causam meam*. He then kissed the ground and made the

---

109. Kendall, Paul Murray, *Richard III* (W.W. Norton & Company, New York, 1955). pp.410-11.

Right: Mill Bay where Henry Tudor landed on 7 August 1485. (Courtesy of Alan Hughes; www.geograph.org.uk)

Below: Commemorative plaque at Mill Bay. (Courtesy of Alan Hughes; www.geograph.org.uk)

MILL BAY MEMORIAL

Mill Bay where Henry Tudor landed on 7 August 1485. (Courtesy of Tony Atkin; www.geograph.org.uk)

sign of the cross across his chest. Henry Tudor and his troops ascended the gulley to the cliff, where a beachhead was established. Leaving a contingent to defend Mill Bay, Henry led an assault force 2km northwards to Dale Castle. The rebels were not opposed and Henry spent the night at Dale. It was here that he rewarded some of his supporters with knighthoods, including Philibert de Chandée, commander of his rebels. During the following morning he began the march through west Wales, where he gathered further support from Welsh mercenaries before heading east into England, where he was joined by Scottish and English supporters.

A plaque commemorates the landing of Henry Tudor at Mill Bay on 7 August 1485 and the campaign that was concluded fifteen days later with his victory at Bosworth.

86
Henry Tudor House, Shrewsbury

Henry VII was reputed to have lodged in this building during his journey to Bosworth in 1485.

On his journey from Mill Bay through Wales, Henry Tudor was increasing the size of his army with Welsh mercenaries and English supporters joining its ranks. However, Henry had expected more troops to rally to his banner and was disappointed. Henry was eager to engage in battle before the king could assemble more troops.

Ten days after landing at Mill Bay, on 17 August, Henry arrived in Shrewsbury. The gates of the town were locked when he arrived during the evening and he had to be let in by the bailiff, John Mitton. Henry Tudor stayed in this half-timbered building,

Henry Tudor House, Shrewsbury. (Courtesy of Stephen Richards; www.geograph.org.uk)

which had been built during the early 1400s. Prior to his arrival, Henry had sent messages to his mother, Lady Margaret Beaufort, and his stepfather, Thomas Baron Stanley, for help. He also wrote to Sir William Stanley, Reginald Bray and to all those individuals who had pledged support instructing them to meet him at Shrewsbury with men and money, from where they would then march on to London. It was here within this building that Henry waited for responses for his appeals for men and money for his campaign. While in Shrewsbury, he received letters of support, but that was not substantiated with men to join his ranks. Bray brought money, while Sir William Stanley had actually been sent to Wales to intercept Henry Tudor's invasion force. Lord Stanley was encamped east of Shrewsbury, while Sir William was positioned north-east of the town; however, they were not prepared to commit to Henry's cause at this stage. They deterred Henry from marching to London and instead urged him to confront Richard III. The Stanleys had a reputation of declaring their allegiance to the winning side. Lord Stanley was also concerned that his son was held in the king's custody and feared for his safety.

87

Blue Boar Inn, Leicester

The site where Richard III spent the night of 20–21 August 1485 before proceeding to Bosworth.

Six armies descended upon Leicester during August 1485. Richard was heading from Nottingham from the north, followed by calvary belonging to Henry Percy, 4th Duke of Northumberland. Two armies belonging to Thomas, 1st Baron Stanley, and Sir William Stanley were approaching from the west, followed by forces led by Henry Tudor. John Howard, 1st Duke of Norfolk, assembled men from the South Midlands. The armies of Stanley and Northumberland held the balance of power and their support would decide the victor. Richard arrived in Leicester before nightfall and stayed at the Blue Boar Inn.

The Blue Boar, originally named the White Boar, was built during the fifteenth century and was the primary coaching inn in Leicester where merchants and noblemen stayed. Richard III wanted to engage with Henry Tudor to prevent him from reaching London and headed towards him. He convened a council of war to decide the next course of action. Richard, Norfolk and his son, Thomas Howard, Earl of Surrey, decided to wait in Leicester a further day to assess whether Northumberland and his rebels would alter their direction.

Supporters of Richard III arrived in Leicester during 20 August, including Sir Robert Brackenbury, who arrived with a contingent from the Tower of London. He reported that Cardinal Thomas Bourchier, Archbishop of Canterbury, and Sir Walter Hungerford, who were ordered to join Richard, had defected from his party at Stony Stratford and were heading to join Henry Tudor. During the afternoon, Richard received intelligence from his scouts that the Stanleys had encamped 10 miles west of Leicester and that Henry Tudor was 3 miles behind their position. Richard decided that his army would move during the following day with the intention of engaging in battle with Henry and to see where the loyalty of the Stanleys was placed. During the evening of 21 August, Northumberland joined Richard at Leicester.

The room in which Richard spent the night at the Blue Boar Inn was described as 'a gloomy chamber'. He had brought his own bed from Nottingham Castle because 'he slept ill in strange beds.' Confident of victory, the bed was left at the inn ready for Richard's return after the battle. The bed is now on display at Donington-le-Heath Manor House, near Coalville, Leicestershire. Richard did not return and it is alleged that the proprietor of the inn rapidly

Above left: Site of the Blue Boar Inn at Leicester Central Travelodge in Highcross Street, Leicester. (Author's collection)

Above right: Richard III depicted at the Blue Boar Inn by John Fulleylove in his painting, 1880. (via Author)

changed its name to the Blue Boar Inn, the Blue Boar being the badge of the Earl of Oxford, a Lancastrian supporter of Henry Tudor.

The Blue Boar Inn was situated in the centre of Leicester, which made it an ideal assembly point for Richard to rally his army before marching to Bosworth. On 21 August 1485 trumpets heralded the departure of Richard III's royal army. Leicester Central Travelodge was built on the site of the Blue Boar Inn and there is an information panel that commemorates Richard III's association with the site.

88

Bow Bridge, Leicester

The current cast-iron bridge built in 1863 replaced the medieval stone bridge used by Richard III on his journey to Bosworth.

It was called the Bow Bridge because the large arches that spanned the bridge were built in the shape of a bow. On 21 August 1485, Richard III passed over the medieval bridge, which crossed the River Soar, as he departed Leicester to meet Henry Tudor at Bosworth.

Soldiers and archers belonging to John Howard, 1st Duke of Norfolk, protected by cavalry were at the vanguard of the Royal Army, followed by Richard III, who was accompanied by Northumberland and Norfolk. These were followed by soldiers from the north and

Eastern end of the Bow Bridge showing Benjamin Broadbent's plaque that incorrectly states that the remains of Richard III were laid near to this spot. (Author's collection)

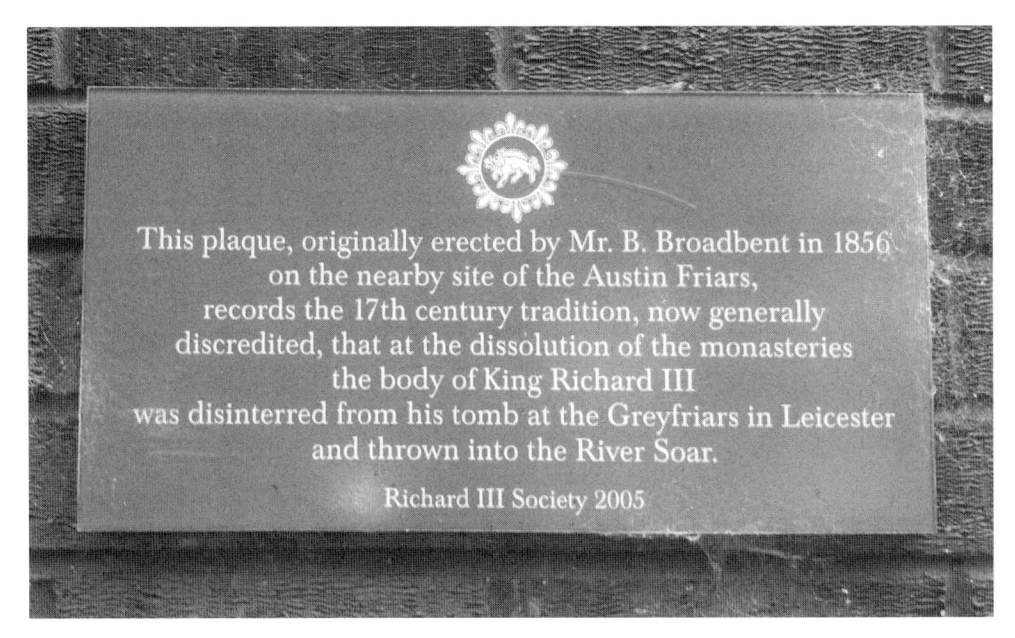

Above: The plaque inaugurated by the Richard III Society that refutes the Broadbent assertion. (Author's collection)

Below: The Bow Bridge, showing the emblems of Richard III, the York and Tudor roses. (Author's collection)

the Midlands. After crossing Bow Bridge, they proceeded westwards towards the Roman-built Watling Street to obstruct Henry Tudor's path to London.

Richard was riding a white horse and dressed in full armour, wearing a golden crown upon his helmet. According to legend, the spur of Richard III struck a part of Bow Bridge as he rode across the bridge. An old woman who was appealing for alms but who was ignored by the king witnessed this happen. She prophesied that when Richard returned to Leicester, his head would strike the bridge at the same spot. On the 22 August his naked corpse, carried on horseback, followed the same route back into the city across the same bridge and the old woman's prophesy came true.

The original medieval bridge was demolished in 1861, but its replacement, built in 1863 in iron, was designed to honour Richard III, with emblems of the Tudor rose, the white rose of York, Richard III's white boar and his motto 'Loyaulte me Lie' (Loyalty Binds Me).

After the dissolution of the monasteries in 1538, there was speculation that the remains of Richard III were exhumed by a disgruntled mob and thrown into the River Soar. In 1856, Benjamin Broadbent, a local builder, erected a plaque at the eastern end of the bridge that stated it was near to the spot where Richard's remains were disposed of. In 2005, the Richard III Society erected a plaque that discredited this claim.

89

King Dick's Well, Bosworth

Richard III is reputed to have drunk from this well.

It is believed that within the vicinity of this spring Richard III's Yorkist army assembled on this high ground known as Ambion Hill on its southern slope, while some historians believe it was further north and close to Sutton Cheney.

In 1577, Raphael Holinshed wrote that: 'King Richard pitched his field on a hill called Anne Beame, refreshed his soldiers and took his rest.' The Reverend Samuel Parr built this cairn in 1813 over the spring from where it is reputed that Richard drank a last drop of water before he went into battle at Bosworth on 22 August 1485. Although the plaque on the cairn states that Richard was killed near this spot, it is believed that he died in marshes a mile south-west of this position near Fen Lane.

It was from Ambion Hill that Richard could see the camp fires of the opposing armies of Henry Tudor and Sir William Stanley, which were encamped on low ground south-west and north-west of Ambion Hill respectively, with Lord Stanley approaching from the south. Henry Tudor was encamped at Merevale Abbey, which was close to Watling Street. According to Croyland, while at Ambion Hill, Richard experienced an unsettled night and his anxieties were prominent on his mind:

> At day-break on the Monday following there were no chaplains present to provide Divine service on behalf of king Richard, nor any breakfast prepared to refresh the flagging spirits of the king; besides, which, as it is generally stated, in the morning he declared that during the night he had seen dreadful visions, and had imagined himself surrounded by a multitude of demons. He consequently presented a countenance which, always attenuated, was on this occasion more livid and ghastly than usual, and asserted that the issue of this day's battle, to whichever side the victory might be granted, would prove the utter destruction of the kingdom of England.[110]

---

110. Riley, *Croyland*, op. cit., p.503.

King Dick's Well. (Author's collection)

Caution must be made when reading Croyland's account, because the writer was not present at the camp and this account was probably based on rumour. It is believed the feeling within the Yorkist camp was that the king was confident, because he paraded in front of his soldiers before the battle. It was from this camp that Richard descended from Ambion Hill to join the battle that was taking place in the vicinity of Fenn Lane.

90

Bosworth Battlefield Site, Fenn Lane, and the Bosworth Boar

The field adjacent to Fenn Lane is believed to be where Richard III fought his last stand at Bosworth. The Bosworth boar, Richard's emblem, was found within the vicinity.

The Bosworth Battlefield Survey that took place during 2009 positioned the actual site of the Battle of the Bosworth astride Fenn Lane, approximately a mile south-west from Ambion Hill and the Bosworth Battlefield Heritage Centre. This silver gilt badge, known as the Bosworth boar, was found by Carl Dawson during that survey. This badge would have been worn by a lord or a knight who fought alongside Richard during the battle. The boar was the emblem of Richard III, and Yorkist knights and noblemen wore it to display their allegiance. It was among other fragments from the battle found during the survey and indicates Richard's proximity to this position during the battle and the location of his last stand.

Henry Tudor had marched 150 miles from Milford Haven in three weeks to reach Merevale Abbey, near Atherstone, Warwickshire. On the morning of 22 August, he led his army down Watling Street before heading north-east along Fenn Lane to confront Richard III and the Yorkist army. Henry was aged 28 and he did not have any experience in commanding soldiers or battle. He had assembled an army comprising 5,000 men, including 2,000 French mercenaries. The soldiers supporting Henry Tudor were inexperienced in battle, exhausted and were about to confront Richard III's Yorkist army that was twice as large, numbering 10,000 men. Richard had proved himself in battle as a leader and a soldier. His army was experienced, well rested and held the high ground, so the odds were against a Lancastrian victory. Richard also brought artillery with him to Bosworth from the Tower of London and from the English garrison in Calais. As mentioned earlier, Richard was an experienced soldier and general who had taken part in the Battles of Barnet and Tewkesbury as well as leading the Scottish campaign. Henry's experience of battle was as a witness of the Battle of Edgcote in 1469, when he was aged 12.

Sir William Stanley had assembled 2,500 men, while Lord Stanley had mustered 3,500, and neither men had declared which side they would join. Instead they held back to wait to see who would likely be the victor and then join their allegiance to them.

Fenn Lane, near Stoke Golding, the actual location of Bosworth battlefield as determined from the battlefield survey in 2009. The photo is looking south-east from Fenn Lane, across the fields of Fenn Lane Farm. Soil was taken from this area and placed in the grave of Richard III when he was reinterred in Leicester Cathedral in 2015. The battle was fought astride Fenn Lane and it was here that round shot and the silver-gilt boar badge was found by the Battlefields Trust, which helped to identify the Bosworth battlefield site. On the horizon can be seen the spire of Stoke Golding Church, which is now known as Crown Hill, where the crown was placed upon the head of Henry VII. (Courtesy of Daveleicuk; via Wikimedia Commons)

Personal testimonies from the Battle of Bosworth do not exist. The battle was fought during the morning of 22 August 1485 and lasted for three hours. Henry Tudor deployed the experienced Earl of Oxford to charge at the Yorkist line with cavalry and infantry, while he followed behind. As Oxford's men came within range of Yorkist cannon and archers, he turned his men northwards to assault Richard's right flank, where they engaged with the Yorkist vanguard led by Norfolk. Henry Tudor's soldiers held their ground and killed Norfolk in the battle, while his son was captured and later imprisoned.

As the battle continued, Henry's army came close to defeat. As Henry rode towards Sir William Stanley's men with a small party, he was attacked by Richard with 100 men at a position believed to be within the vicinity of Fenn Lane. Richard came so close to Henry Tudor that he killed William Brandon, his standard bearer. Henry never forgot Brandon's loyalty, for he raised his young son, Charles, within the royal household and he would become a close friend and confidante of Henry VIII.

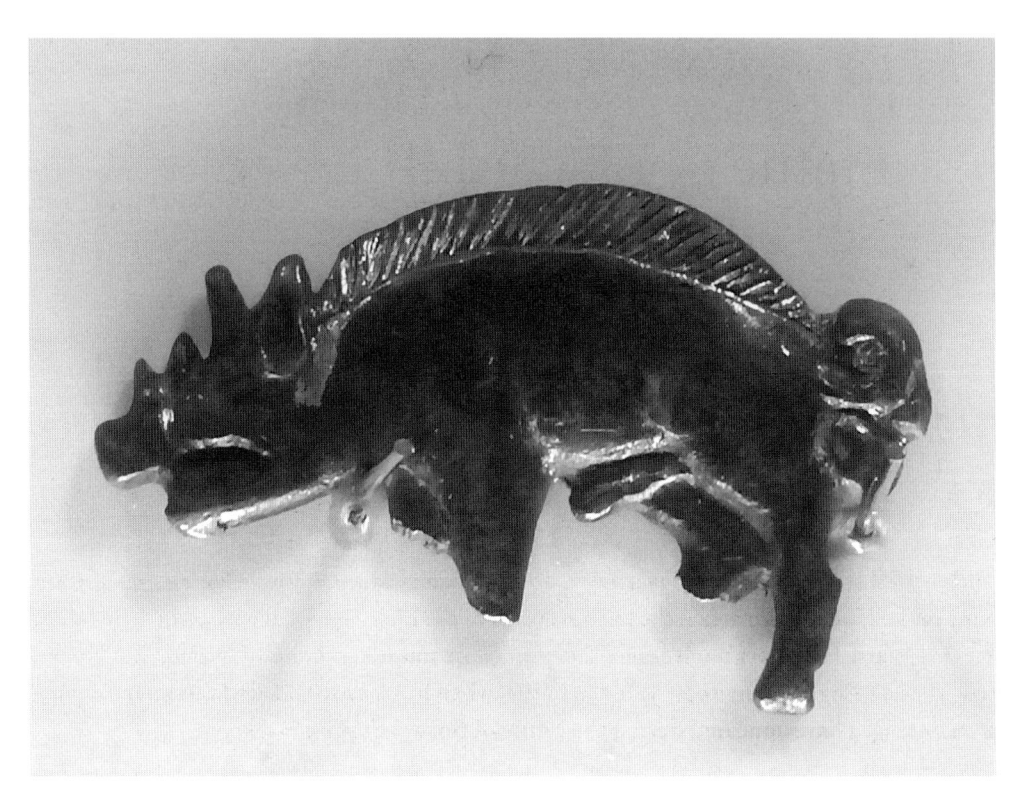

The Bosworth Boar, found in a field adjacent to Fenn Lane. (Author's collection)

Richard also brought Sir John Cheney (also known as Cheyne), who was Henry's personal bodyguard, to the ground. This was a remarkable feat for Richard, who was small in stature, for Cheney was 6ft 8in tall. Despite Richard's valour, Stanley decided to support Henry Tudor and the balance of power tipped against the Yorkists. Richard III became surrounded and was unhorsed, but he continued to fight.

91

Statue of Richard III, Leicester

Close to Leicester Cathedral stands the statue of Richard III. It depicts the last Plantagenet King with drawn sword and crown in hand.

Richard III is the most controversial of the English medieval monarchs. He was the last king of the House of York and the last sovereign of the Plantagenet dynasty, which had ruled for 331 years. His short reign lasted two years, one month and twenty-eight days. He was also the last English king to be killed in battle, when he was aged 32, and this statue depicts how he might have appeared during the Battle of Bosworth at his last stand.

The inscription on the statue affirms that he was 'a good lawmaker for the ease and solace of the common people … piteously slain fighting manfully in the thickest press of the enemy'.

According to Dominic Mancini, 'such was his renown in warfare, that whenever a difficult and dangerous policy had to be undertaken it would be entrusted to his discretion and his general-ship. By these arts Richard acquired the favour of the people, and avoided the jealousy of the Queen [Elizabeth] from whom he lived far separated.'[111]

This statue depicts Richard III as the warrior king, who had distinguished himself in battle at Barnet and Tewkesbury. It shows the manner in which he died, defending his crown. The *Croyland Chronicle* confirmed that 'for while fighting, and not in the act of flight, the said king Richard was pierced with numerous deadly wounds, and fell in the field like a brave and most valiant prince'.[112]

An English king had not been killed in battle since Harold was killed at the Battle of Hastings in 1066. Despite being commissioned by Henry VII to write the *History of England*, Polydore Vergil commended and acknowledged the courage of his opponent, writing that 'King Richard, alone, was killed, fighting manfully in the thickest press of his enemies'.[113]

---

111. Cheetham, op. cit., p.91.

112. Riley, *Croyland*, op. cit., p.504.

113. Ellis, Sir Henry, *Three books of Polydore Vergil's English history, comprising the reigns of Henry VI, Edward IV, and Richard III* (J.B. Nichols and Sons, London, 1844), p.224.

James Butler, R.A., was commissioned by the Richard III Society to sculpture this fine depiction of Richard III as the warrior king. It was gifted to the people of Leicester and unveiled by Princess Alice, Duchess of Gloucester, during July 1980.

Statue of Richard III close to Leicester Cathedral. (Author's collection)

92

Sundial Memorial, Bosworth

Henry Tudor is crowned Henry VII.

The Sundial Memorial at the Bosworth Heritage Visitor Centre comprises a crown in the centre surrounded by three thrones representing the three main participants, Henry Tudor, Earl of Richmond, Richard III and Lord Stanley. This image shows the throne of Henry Tudor with his Royal Standard.

The Sundial Memorial at Bosworth represents a significant turning point in English history. It signified the end of the Plantagenet era and the emergence of a new royal dynasty, the Tudors, which would govern for the following 118 years. Transformations implemented by the Tudors would last into the twenty-first century. Through Henry VIII, England broke away from Catholicism and established the Church of England. The Protestantism was adopted as the national religion during the reign of Elizabeth I. England's dominance of the seas, the establishment of trade routes and the strengthening of its navy enabled it to start building an empire.

Sundial Memorial. (Author's collection)

Crowning of Henry VII after his victory at Bosworth. (Author's collection)

Henry Tudor was crowned at Stoke Golding, 1 mile south of the Bosworth Heritage Visitor Centre. Sir William Stanley found the body of Richard III on the Bosworth battlefield, recovered the crown from his helmet and placed it upon the head of Henry Tudor. Vergil wrote of the moment of Henry Tudor's victory in his *History of England*:

> Henry, after the victory obtained, gave further thanks unto Almighty God for the same; then after replenished with joy incredible, he got himself unto the next hill, where, after he had commended his soldiers, and commanded to cure the wounded, and to bury them that were slain, he gave unto the nobility and gentlemen immortal thanks, promising that he would be mindful of their benefits, all which mean while the soldiers cried God save king Henry, God save king Henry! and with heart and hand uttered all the show of joy that might be; which when Thomas Stanley did see, he set anon king Richard's crown, which was found among the spoil in the field upon his head, as though he had been already by commandment of the people, proclaimed king after the manner of his ancestors, and that was the first sign of prosperity.[114]

---

114. Ellis, Sir Henry, *Three books of Polydore Vergil's English history, comprising the reigns of Henry VI, Edward IV, and Richard III*. (J.B. Nichols and Sons, London 1844), p.226.

93

The Two Kings' Plaque, Leicester

During 21 and 22 August 1485, the city of Leicester received two English sovereigns.

There was just a five-year age difference between Henry VII, 28, and Richard III, who was 33. The two men had never met, for Henry had lived a large part of his adult life in exile in Brittany.

A plaque on the wall of the Judge's Lodgings in Castle View Leicester bearing the arms of Richard III and Henry VII reads as follows:

> This is to commemorate the occasions five hundred years ago when the people of Leicester greeted and honoured two kings of England within two days. RICHARD III in his solemn departure from the town on the 21 of August 1485 to do battle for his kingdom and HENRY VII on his arrival in the evening of the 22 of August 1485 from his victorious field near Market Bosworth bringing in his train the body of the vanquished Richard III.

Richard III was last seen alive by the people of Leicester, so it was important to Henry VII that his body be brought back to the city so that his corpse could be seen to prevent future imposters claiming to be the dead monarch and challenging him.

According to Croyland:

> through this battle was obtained for the entire kingdom, and the body of the said king Richard being found among the dead. Many other insults were also heaped upon it, and, not in the accordance with the laws of humanity, a halter being thrown round the neck, it was carried to Leicester; while the new king also proceeded to the place, graced with the crown which he had so gloriously won.[115]

---

115. Riley, op. cit., p.504.

The Two Kings' Plaque, Leicester. (Author's collection)

Some of Richard's officers captured on the battlefield at Bosworth were brought to Leicester. Among them was William Catesby, an advisor to Richard, who was sent to Brittany to sabotage support for Henry Tudor. Catesby was beheaded alongside John Bracher, who had betrayed Henry when he alerted Richard to his landing at Mill Bay.

Henry VII felt insecure about his weak claim to the throne and in order to ensure that his subjects could perceive that his accession was lawful the public relations exercise to tarnish the reputation of Richard III began in Leicester. Henry claimed that his reign had begun the day prior to the Battle of Bosworth, so that the Yorkist attack upon him was an act of treason. Henry chose to celebrate his victory at Bosworth at a banquet held in Coventry on 24 August 1485 and he stayed at the home of the local mayor, Robert Onley, before returning to Leicester.

94

Turret gateway entrance to Leicester Castle

The body of Richard III was most likely brought through this gateway.

Built in 1423, this archway was part of the fortified gate, which had a turreted house above it, that formed the southern entrance to Leicester Castle. It separated the castle from the religious district, known as Newarke.

This gateway was one of two entrances into this district, the other being the Newarke Gateway, which is now known as the Magazine Gateway. A portcullis would have prevented access to the castle and the groove can still be seen. Richard III is recorded to have visited the castle weeks after he was crowned in July 1483, because a letter exists that he wrote, signed 'from my castle of Leicester'. It was probable that he would use this entrance to enter the north entrance of the inner bailey and it was likely that his corpse was brought into the Newarke district through the Turret Gateway, where his remains would have been displayed at the Church of Annunciation. The Turret Gateway is also known as Rupert's Gateway, after the Royalist commander Prince Rupert, who captured Leicester during the English Civil War in 1645.

Once in the Newarke district, Richard's naked corpse was displayed in the Church of the Blessed Virgin Mary to prove to the people of England that he was dead. After three days, the body was removed by the Grey Friars to be buried within their own church.

Turret Gateway looking south through the arch via which the corpse of Richard III passed. (Author's collection)

95

A royal grave, Greyfriars, Leicester

Richard III is buried at Greyfriars.

Greyfriars Friary was constructed in Leicester during the twelfth century and became the home of the Franciscan order, who were known as the Grey Friars after the colour of their habits. Greyfriars Friary consisted of a church, cloisters, a chapter house and accommodation for the friars.

Franciscan friars of Leicester took Richard's body away for a simple Christian burial in the choir of their church at Greyfriars. By interring his remains in the choir, he was honoured, but the location was concealed to prevent his grave becoming a Yorkist shrine or a place of pilgrimage. According to Polydore Vergil:

> the body of King Richard, naked of all clothing, and laid upon a horseback with the arms and legs hanging down on both sides, was brought to the abbey of the monks Franciscans at Leicester, a miserable spectacle in good sooth, but not unworthy for the man's life and there was buried two days after without any pomp or solemn funeral.[116]

It is not certain whether the friars acted under the orders of Henry or their own initiative. It is probable that he would have wanted the place of Richard's burial to be known, to ensure that imposters did not try to continue to champion the Yorkist claim to the throne. A decade after Richard's death, during 1494, Henry ordered that the grave be marked, possibly as an act to unify the country.

Greyfriars Friary was dissolved and demolished under the orders of Henry VIII in 1538 during the reformation and the grave of Richard III was lost and unmarked. The site was redeveloped with various constructions at numerous times over the following five centuries. The site would eventually become the offices of Leicester City Council and a car park, which would complicate the search for the grave of Richard III. All that remains of Greyfriars Friary is a small section of wall that is located next to the attendant's hut in the car park near to the Cathedral end of New Street.

---

116. Vergil, op. cit., p.226.

The grave of Richard III. (Author's collection)

Philippa Langley and John Ashdown-Hill founded the *Looking for Richard Project* with the aim of finding Richard III's burial site. They raised the necessary funds and commissioned an archaeological team at the University of Leicester to excavate the Greyfriars site. The search began in Leicester City Council car park on 25 August 2012, the 527th anniversary of his burial at Greyfriars. A human leg bone was found in the first trench dug on the first day of the dig, beneath the letter R that marked reserved parking. This indicated that a grave had been found, but with little information the remains were covered and during the following two weeks medieval ruins were discovered that determined Greyfriars Friary had been found. An application for an exhumation licence was submitted and granted. Interest was focused onto the leg bones, which were found on the first day of the dig.

During 4 and 5 September 2012, Dr Jo Appleby excavated the remainder of the skeleton, which was found to have had a curved spine. Supporters of Richard III had argued that Shakespeare's depiction of a hunchbacked monarch was a myth and he would not have been able to ride a horse or function as a soldier, but discovery of his skeleton indicated that he did have a deformed spine. This was a probable contender for Richard III and the remains were sent for further investigation to the University of Leicester. After Carbon-14 dating analysis that determined that the remains originated in the late fifteenth century and a DNA match between the remains and Michael Ibsen, a living descendent of Richard III, it was confirmed on 4 February 2013 that they belonged to the king. The revelation became a global sensation, with the media dubbing Richard III the 'king in the car park'. The burial place was preserved in the King Richard III Visitor Centre, which was opened in Leicester in July 2014.

96

Skeleton of Richard III

The research conducted upon the skeletal remains of Richard III have provided an insight into the type of wounds inflicted upon thousands of other soldiers during medieval battles such as the Wars of the Roses.

The skeleton was an adult male and the spinal curves indicated that he suffered from scoliosis. It is believed that Richard began to show signs of suffering from scoliosis during his adolescence, which would have caused one shoulder to be higher than the other and corresponds with John Rous' description of Richard. 'He was small of stature, with a short face and unequal shoulders, the right higher and the left lower.'[117] Rous was a Warwickshire priest who had seen Richard during his progress in 1483.

Various CT scans indicated that this man had died between the age of 30 to 34. Carbon dating analysis confirmed that the date of death was between 1455 and 1548. Isotopic analysis confirmed that the man ate a high-status diet consistent of someone of high standing such as a king. DNA samples were extracted from the skeleton and tested against samples from two living descendants of the sovereign, which matched. The scientific analysis obtained enabled the team at the University of Leicester to confirm that the remains of Richard III had been found.

Eight weapon injuries were confirmed upon the skull, which reconciles with contemporary accounts that suggested that he was killed by a head wound. The evidence indicated that Richard had removed his protective helmet and had sustained a puncture wound close to his nose and a blade cut to the lower jaw. It is acknowledged that a Welshman brandishing a war bill was responsible for killing the king and he may have been responsible for inflicting a stab injury to the top of the skull. This wound would have been made by a heavy spiked weapon that would have needed to have been sufficiently strong to penetrate through Richard's helmet and skull. It could have been made by a dagger if Richard had removed his helmet. There were also small abrasions to the sides of the skull, which would have been incurred if Richard had removed his helmet. There were a further two wounds to the rear of the lower skull. The larger one was caused by a bladed

---

117. British Library: Cotton MS Vespian A XII.

weapon such as a halberd, while the other is a smaller stab wound. Both would have killed the king. Richard also received a slice wound to the pelvis and sword or knife wound that entered his buttock and reached a rib. These may have been inflicted after his death, when his armour had been removed, and are classed as post-death humiliation injuries.

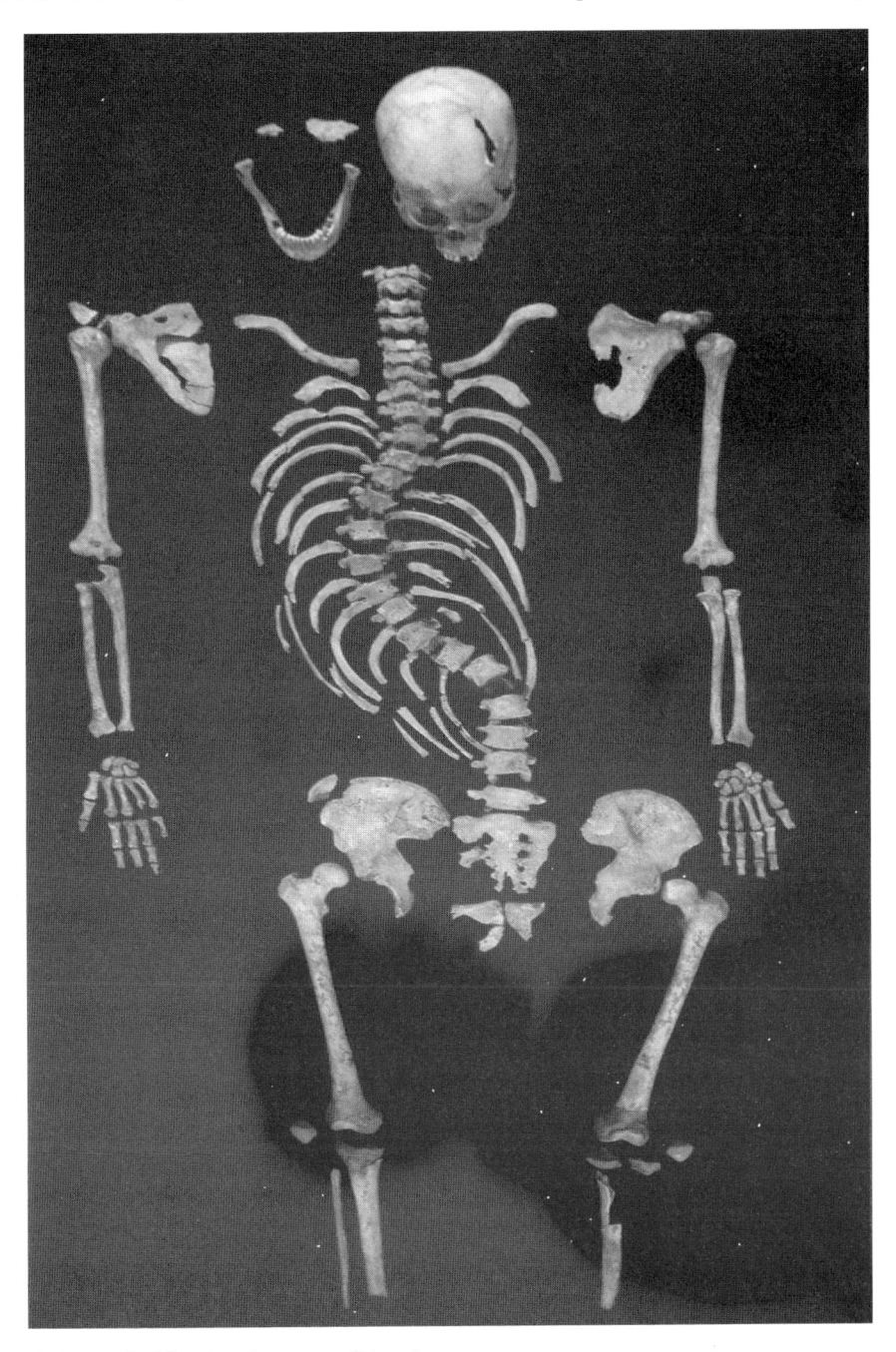

Skeleton of Richard III. (PA Images/Alamy)

97

Tomb of Richard III

Richard III was reburied within Leicester Cathedral, less than 100m from his original burial place in Greyfriars Church.

Construction of St Martin's Church was begun by the Normans 900 years ago. The church spire was built in the nineteenth century. The church was expanded during the thirteenth and fourteenth centuries, when it evolved into the civic church with strong links to guilds and merchants who were associated with the Guildhall, which is close by. During the nineteenth century, architect Raphael Brandon rebuilt the church and added the 220ft spire that can be seen today. The Diocese of Leicester was re-established in 1927 and St Martin's Church was consecrated as Leicester Cathedral.

Cabinetmaker Michael Ibsen, the seventeenth-generation nephew of Richard III, built the lead-lined oak coffin in which his distinguished ancestor was interred Ibsen was one of the two living descendants whose DNA matched with the skeletal remains, which confirmed that the remains were King Richard III. A symbolic procession began on 22 March 2015 that brought his remains to his final resting place at Leicester Cathedral. The cortège first stopped at Fenn Lane Farm, which is close to where it is believed Richard III was killed, where a private ceremony took place. The procession then proceeded to Dadlington, where many of the soldiers who fell during that battle were buried, and then on to St James' Church in Sutton Cheney, where it is supposed that Richard established his camp and heard mass during the night prior to the battle. The procession then continued to the Bosworth Battlefield Heritage Centre, where a further ceremony was held officiated by Tim Stevens, Bishop of Leicester. A twenty-one-cannon salute paid homage to Richard III as the hearse departed for Leicester. Civil dignitaries met the cortège at Bow Bridge before it was taken to St Nicholas Church, where the coffin was transferred onto a horse-driven hearse. The people of Leicester lined the streets in solemn silence as the coffin was taken to the cathedral. White roses were thrown onto the coffin as a mark of respect. Twenty thousand people passed by the coffin of Richard III, with military veterans providing the guard of honour in Leicester Cathedral for the following three days.

The service of the reinterment of Richard III took place at Leicester Cathedral on 26 March 2015 led by the Reverend Justin Welby, Archbishop of Canterbury, and the Dean of Leicester

Final resting place of Richard III in Leicester Cathedral. (Author's collection)

in the presence of the Duke and Duchess of Gloucester and Sophie, Countess of Wessex. His tomb lies facing the chapel of Christ the King, commemorating Christ's death and resurrection, and faces the resurrection east window.

The tomb was carved from Swaledale limestone. Richard III's name, motto, dates of his birth and death, alongside his coat of arms, are inscribed on the marble plinth, and his body rests with a dignity that he was denied until 530 years after his death.

98

Rose Window, York Minster

Constructed after 1484, the red and white roses in the Rose Window at York Minster commemorated the marriage of Henry VII to Elizabeth of York and the union of the Houses of Lancaster and York.

The defeat of Richard III at Bosworth in 1485 was a decisive moment in English history. It brought an end to the Plantagenet line of succession and the beginning of a new, powerful dynasty that would have a significant impact upon the nation. Henry VII was crowned in Westminster Abbey on 30 October 1485 and this brought peace and stability to the nation. Henry VII was not a natural Lancastrian successor, so he had to protect the throne that he had seized. In order to consolidate and legitimise his position he had to blacken the character of Richard III. As king, he repealed the *Act of Titulus Regius* (Royal Title) that was passed through parliament in 1484 and gave the title of King of England to Richard III, also ratifying the declaration made in Parliament during the previous year that the marriage of Edward IV and Elizabeth of York was invalid and that their children were illegitimate. Henry VII acknowledged that Edward V was his predecessor and that the children of Edward IV were legitimate. On 18 January 1486, Henry married Elizabeth of York at Westminster Abbey in a ceremony officiated by Cardinal Bourchier, Archbishop of Canterbury. Elizabeth was the eldest child of Edward IV, and with no surviving brothers, she had a strong claim to the throne in her own right. She gave birth to their first child, Arthur, on 20 September 1486 and was crowned queen on 25 November 1487.

The marriage of Henry Tudor to the daughter of Edward IV unified the Houses of York and Lancaster and united the country. The Rose Window was constructed in the South Transept of York Minster to celebrate the marriage and union and contains seventy-three panels and 40,000 pieces of stained glass. It depicts the Tudor rose, which features the merging of the red Tudor rose that first appeared in 1485 with the white rose of York. That made the Rose Window a powerful symbol of the Tudor dynasty. It was also a step in the healing process for the opposing factions that fought the Wars of the Roses. The Rose Window sustained serious damage in a fire at York Minster during 1984 that destroyed the roof.

After supressing one final act of Yorkist rebellion at Stoke Field in 1487, Henry VII would stabilise the country. He built on the work done by his predecessor and retained the well-established councils that governed northern England and Wales on the sovereign's behalf. Henry

Above: The Rose Window in the South Transept of York Minster. (Cynthia Liang/Shutterstock)

Right: Exterior view of the Rose Window and South Transept of York Minister. (Author's collection)

also granted Justices of the Peace Royal Authority, establishing the first state-administered judicial system. Henry also brought prosperity at the expense of high taxation and austerity, which was not popular among his subjects. Arranging the marriage of his daughter, Margaret, to the Scottish King James IV in 1503 would ultimately lead to the unification of England and Scotland when James VI ascended the English throne in 1603.

99

Gatehouse of Richmond Palace

Henry VII died at Richmond Palace.

All that remains of Richmond Palace, which was built along the southern bank of the River Thames, is the Outer Gateway and a small part of the house known as the Old Palace, which is on the western perimeter of Richmond Green. This gatehouse formed the principal access to Richmond Palace on the landward side. It comprised a large opening that once held a pair of large doors (the surviving hinge pins still exist) and a now-blocked entrance to the right of the gatehouse. The arms of Henry VII, restored in 1976, are carved above the entrance. Significantly relevant to the Tudor dynasty, a plaque on the wall confirms 'Richmond Palace. Residence of King Henry VII, King Henry VIII, Queen Elizabeth I'.

Richmond was used as a royal residence from the time of Henry I, when there was a manor house on this site. Edward III transformed this building into the Palace of Shene, where he died in 1377. When Anna, the wife of his successor, Richard II, died here in 1394, the king, being so distraught in his bereavement, ordered the destruction of the

Gatehouse of Richmond Palace. (Author's collection)

RICHMOND

Above: Richmond Palace drawn by Wenceslaus Hollar in 1638. (Author's collection)

Right: Coat of arms of Henry VII above the landward entrance to Richmond Palace. (Author's collection)

palace. Henry V started construction of a new palace, which was completed by Henry VI. This became a favourite residence of Henry VII but it was destroyed in a fire during Christmas 1497. The king immediately ordered the construction of another palace on the same site and it took four years to build.

Henry VII died of tuberculosis at Richmond Palace on 21 April 1509 aged 52. Thomas Platter visited Richmond Palace in 1599 and he was told 'it was according to his command that after his decease, his intestines were slung full of blood against the wall of a chamber in the palace, as a symbol that he conquered the kingdom by force, slaying Richard III who had usurped the realm in battle. Indeed, many traces of blood were pointed out to us in one room.'[118]

---

118. Williams, Clare, *Thomas Platters Travels 1599* (Jonathan Cape, London, 1937), p.227.

100

Tomb of Henry VII and Elizabeth Tudor

Henry VII died on 21 April 1509 and was buried at Westminster Abbey.

After reigning for twenty-four years, Henry VII died from tuberculosis at Richmond Palace on 21 April 1509. Being the first monarch of the Tudor dynasty, he had brought peace and stability to the nation after the savagery of the Wars of the Roses.

In accordance with his wishes, Henry VII was buried in a vault beneath the Lady's Chapel in Westminster Abbey. He had spent large sums of money to fund the building of the Lady's Chapel, which began in 1503 to accommodate the burial of his wife, Elizabeth of York, who died during childbirth that same year. The chapel was designed by Sir Reginald Bray, the person who had retrieved the crown of Richard III from Bosworth Field. Henry VII and Elizabeth of York were the first monarchs to be buried in a vault beneath Westminster Abbey. All previous monarchs buried within the abbey were in tombs above the floor. In 1512, Henry VIII commissioned the Italian sculptor Pieter Torrigiano to design and construct a tomb dedicated to his parents.

In contrast to the minimal, paltry interment of Richard III at Greyfriars, Henry VII was buried with pomp and ceremony at Westminster Abbey. The traditional royal place of burial close to the Shrine of Edward the Confessor was full to capacity. Richard III would have appreciated the shortage of burial space for the royal family because when his wife, Anne Neville, was buried in the abbey, her remains were wedged into a position in front of the sedilia, which were stone seats, adjacent to the high altar in an unmarked grave, in front of the Confessor's Chapel. A tablet was later laid on the ground to denote her place of burial. So, during his reign, Henry VII considered where he would be interred and decided to expand Westminster Abbey with a larger burial space, which was called the Lady Chapel.

On 9 May 1509, the embalmed corpse of Henry VII was drawn by chariot from Richmond Palace and taken to St George's Field, south of the River Thames. There it was met by the clergy, before it was transported across the old medieval bridge that spanned the Thames and taken to St Paul's Cathedral, where the Bishop of Rochester conducted mass. The body was then taken to Westminster Abbey for interment during the following day, when a further ceremony was held. At the end of the ceremony a knight rode into the abbey wearing the late king's armour. The armour was removed by monks, who unbuckled it piece by piece and placed the pieces upon the altar. Henry VII, the victor of Bosworth Field and the father of the Tudor dynasty, received the funeral of a warrior, buried among the symbols of medieval aristocracy. He was buried in the Lady's Chapel, which was designed by Sir Reginald Bray. His wife, Elizabeth of York, lies alongside him, and his mother, Lady Margaret Beaufort, who outlived him by two months, was also buried within the chapel.

The tomb not only serves as Henry VIII's tribute to his parents, but it symbolises the union of the Houses of York and Lancaster and the end of the Wars of the Roses. England had been torn apart by thirty years of bloodshed, but after Henry VII defeated the Yorkist Richard III at the Battle of Bosworth on 22 August 1485, in an attempt to unify the nation and prevent further conflict he married Elizabeth of York on 18 January 1486. The tomb is a visual symbol signifying the birth of the Tudor dynasty and the legacy of Henry VII, a legacy that Henry VIII wanted to maintain and continue. A legacy that could only be continued by a male heir.

Tomb of Henry VII and Elizabeth of York at Westminster Abbey. (Copyright Dean and Chapter of Westminster)

Bibliography

Anonymous, *The Chronicles of the White Rose of York* (James Bohn, London, 1845).

Ashdown-Hill, John, *The Last Days of Richard III and the fate of his DNA* (The History Press, 2010).

Ashdown-Hill, John, *The Mythology of Richard III* (Amberley, Gloucestershire, 2015).

Bayley, John, *The History & Antiquities of the Tower of London* (Jennings and Chaplin, London 1830).

Borman, Tracy, The Story of the Tower of London (Merrill, London, 2015).

Brand, Paul, Curry Anne, Horrox, Rosemary, Martin, Geoffrey, Ormrod, Mark, Philips, Seymour, Given-Wilson, Chris, ed, Parliament Rolls of Medieval England (Woodbridge, 2005).

Brooke, Richard, *Visits to Fields of Battle in England of the Fifteenth Century* (J.R. Smith, London 1857).

Brown, Rawdon Lubbock, *Calendar of state papers and manuscripts, relating to English affairs existing in the archives and collection of Venice, and in other libraries of northern Italy, Volume 1, 1202-1509* (Longman, London, 1864).

Bruce, James, *History of the Arrival of Edward VI* (Camden Society, London, 1838)

Edgar, J.G. *The Wars of the Roses,* (Published London 1859).

Carson, Annette, *Domenico Mancini de occupatione regni Anglie* (Imprimis Imprimatur, Horstead, 2021).

Cheetham, Anthony, *Life & Times of Richard III,* (Weidenfeld and Nicolson Limited, 1972)

Christie, Mabel E, *Henry VI* (Houghton Mifflin Company, Boston & New York, 1922)

Commines, Philippe de, *The Memoirs of Philippe de Commines* (G. Bell, London 1877).

Davies, Rev, John. Ed., *An English Chronicle of the Reigns of Richard II, Henry IV, Henry V and Henry VI written before 1471* (Camden Society, 1856).

Davies, J, *The History of England, from the accession of Henry III to the death of Richard III (1216-1485)* (Philip & Son, London, 1875).

Edgar, J.G., *The Wars of the Roses,* Harpers & Brothers, New York).

Ellis, Sir Henry, *Three books of Polydore Vergil's English history, comprising the reigns of Henry VI, Edward IV, and Richard III.* (J.B. Nichols and Sons, London 1844),

Fabyan, Robert, *The New Chronicles of England and France* (Longman, London, 1811).

Gairdner, James, *The Paston Letters 1422-1509 A.D. Volume One* (Public Records Office, London, 1872)

Gairdner, James, *The Historical Collections of a Citizen of London in the Fifteenth Century* (Camden Society, 1876).
Gairdner, James, *The Life & Reign of Richard III* (Cambridge University Press, 1898)
Gairdner, James, *Three Fifteenth Century Chronicles* (Camden Society, 1880).
Gairdner, James, *William Gregory's Chronicle of London* (Camden Society, 1876).
Hall, Edward, *Hall's Chronicle: Henry IV to Henry VIII* (First Published 1548, J. Johnson, London, 1809)
Halstead, Caroline A, *Richard III*, Volume I & II, (Longman, London 1844).
Hicks, Michael, *Richard III* (The History Press, Stroud, 2001).
Hinds, A.B., *Calendar of Milanese Papers: Calendar of State Papers and Manuscripts, relating to English affairs, existing in the Archives and Collections of Milan, Vol. I*, (London, 1912).
Hookham, Dr Mary Anne, The Life & Times of Margaret of Anjou, Volume I and II (Tinsley Brothers, London, 1872).
James, M.E., *Henry VI, A Reprint of John Blacman's Memoir* (University of Cambridge, 1919).
Jones, Dan, *The Hollow Crown* (Faber & Faber, London, 2014).
Kendall, Paul Murray, *Richard III* (W.W. Norton & Company, New York, 1955).
Kingsford, Charles, *Chronicles of London*, (Clarendon Press, Oxford, 1905).
Langley, Philippa, Jones, Michael, *The Search for Richard III, The King's Grave* (John Murray, 2013).
Leland, John, The *Itinerary of John Leland in or about the years 1535-1543, Volume I* (George Bell & Sons, London, 1907).
License, Amy, *Richard III: The Road to Leicester* (Amberley, Stroud, 2014).
Monstrelet, Enguerrand de, *The Chronicles of Enguerrand de Monstrelet* (H.G. Bohn, London 1853).
More, Sir Thomas, *The History of King Richard III* (Cambridge University Press, 1883).
Mowat, R.B., The Wars of the Roses 1377-1471 (Crosby Lockwood & Son, London, 1914).
Ramsay, Sir James, *Lancaster & York* (Clarendon Press, Oxford, 1892).
Riley, Henry T., *Ingulph's Chronicle of the Abbey of Croyland* (George Bell & Sons, London, 1908).
Smith, Philip & Wright, Arnold, *Parliament Past & Present* (Hutchinson & Co., London, 1902).
Stevenson, Joseph, *Letters & Papers of Henry VI* (Longman, London, 1861)
Stratford, Laurence, *Edward IV* (Pitman & Sons, London, 1910).
Stow, John, *A Survey of London* (The Clarendon Press, London, 1908).
Twemlow, Francis Randle, *The Battle of Blore Heath* (Whitehead Printers, Wolverhampton, 1912).
Vergil, Polydore, *English History Comprising the Reigns of Henry VI, Edward IV and Richard III* (J.B. Nichols & Sons, London 1844).
Warkworth, John, *A Chronicle of the first thirteen years of the reign of King Edward the Fourth* (J.B. Nichols and Son, London, 1839).

Wavrin, John de, *A Collection of Chronicle and Ancient Histories of Great Britain, now called England*
Vol. 3 (London, 1864–87).
Williams, Clare, *Thomas Platters Travels 1599*, (Jonathan Cape, London 1937.
Winston, James E., *English Towns in the Wars of the Roses* (Princeton University Press, 1921)